the unbeatable
To All the Squirrels I've Loved Before

COLLECTION EDITOR: **JENNIFER GRÜNWALD**
ASSISTANT MANAGING EDITOR: **MAIA LOY**
ASSISTANT EDITOR: **CAITLIN O'CONNELL**
EDITOR, SPECIAL PROJECTS: **MARK D. BEAZLEY**
VP PRODUCTION & SPECIAL PROJECTS: **JEFF YOUNGQUIST**
BOOK DESIGNERS: **ADAM DEL RE** WITH **JAY BOWEN**
SVP PRINT, SALES & MARKETING: **DAVID GABRIEL**
EDITOR IN CHIEF: **C.B. CEBULSKI**

THE UNBEATABLE SQUIRREL GIRL VOL. 12: TO ALL THE SQUIRRELS I LOVED BEFORE. Contains material originally published in magazine form as THE UNBEATABLE SQUIRREL GIRL (2015B) #47-50. First printing 2020. ISBN 978-1-302-91724-1. Published by MARVEL WORLDWIDE, INC., a subsidiary of MARVEL ENTERTAINMENT, LLC. OFFICE OF PUBLICATION: 1290 Avenue of the Americas, New York, NY 10104. **Printed in Canada.** KEVIN FEIGE, Chief Creative Officer; DAN BUCKLEY, President, Marvel Entertainment; JOHN NEE, Publisher; JOE QUESADA, EVP & Creative Director; TOM BREVOORT, SVP of Publishing; DAVID BOGART, Associate Publisher & SVP of Talent Affairs; Publishing & Partnership; DAVID GABRIEL, VP of Print & Digital Publishing; JEFF YOUNGQUIST, VP of Production & Special Projects; DAN CARR, Executive Director of Publishing Technology; ALEX MORALES, Director of Publishing Operations; DAN EDINGTON, Managing Editor; SUSAN CRESPI, Production Manager; STAN LEE, Chairman Emeritus. For information regarding advertising in Marvel Comics or on Marvel.com, please contact Vit DeBellis, Custom Solutions & Integrated Advertising Manager, at vdebellis@marvel.com. For Marvel subscription inquiries, please call 888-511-5480. **Manufactured between 1/3/2020 and 2/4/2020 by SOLISCO PRINTERS, SCOTT, QC, CANADA.**

10 9 8 7 6 5 4 3 2 1

To All the Squirrels I've Loved Before

Ryan North
WRITER

Derek Charm
with ***Erica Henderson*** *(#50 song scene)*
ARTISTS

Rico Renzi
COLOR ARTIST

Madeline McGrane *(#47)*, ***Michael Cho*** *(#48)*,
Rico Renzi *(#48)* & ***Evan "Doc" Shaner*** *(#48)*
TRADING CARD ARTISTS

VC's Travis Lanham
LETTERER

Erica Henderson
COVER ART

Michael Allred
LOGO

Sarah Brunstad
ASSOCIATE EDITOR

Wil Moss
EDITOR

SQUIRREL GIRL CREATED BY **WILL MURRAY** & **STEVE DITKO**

47

Doreen Green doesn't just study computer science - she also studies **justice**, thanks to her being born with all the powers of a squirrel **and** all the powers of a girl! With the help of her best friends (human and squirrel), she fights crime and saves Earth on the regular. Her pals call her Doreen - which means you can too! - but if you ever see her in costume, keep her secret identity safe and call her...**The Unbeatable Squirrel Girl!**

Squirrel Girl *in a nutshell*

search! 

#theleader
#doughnatello
#platosdancecave
#factchannel
#greenlight

Squirrel Girl @unbeatablesg
The War of the Realms, huh? What a journey. What an adventure. p.s. Me and my friend saved all of North America for everyone, NBD

Squirrel Girl @unbeatablesg
And what did we learn? Well heck I don't know what YOU learned while the place was overrun by Frost Giants--

Squirrel Girl @unbeatablesg
(who are themselves operating under an unfair absolute monarchy which is really just a hereditary dictatorship, but who knows where they'll be after a year or two of agitating for positive change?)

Squirrel Girl @unbeatablesg
(That's right! Your girl SG doesn't like dictatorships!! Squirrel Girl coming out swinging in favor of DEMOCRACY here, folks)

Squirrel Girl @unbeatablesg
--but getting back to my original post here: I learned that maybe I shouldn't be so quick to judge people who I think are jerks.

Squirrel Girl @unbeatablesg
It's too easy to decide you don't like someone, even when you don't know them, you know? Or you think you know them, but really you don't, because as my friend Brain Drain would say, "THE MINDS OF OTHER PEOPLE ARE A FOREIGN COUNTRY; THEY DO THINGS DIFFERENTLY THERE."

Squirrel Girl @unbeatablesg
(Brain Drain loves his L.P. Hartley, what can I say)

Squirrel Girl @unbeatablesg
Oh man. Reading this over, I don't know. It feels like all I'm saying is just "dOn'T jUdGe a BoOk bY iTs CoVeR!" but it felt more than that, you know?

Squirrel Girl @unbeatablesg
Like you go through life thinking that people around you are jerks, and yeah they are, but there's reasons for that, and often the underlying issues they're dealing with somehow AREN'T solved by you calling them a jerk.

Squirrel Girl @unbeatablesg
And it's not your job to solve everyone else's issues, and it's not your responsibility to fix everyone, even if you could.

Squirrel Girl @unbeatablesg
But you can be kind.

Squirrel Girl @unbeatablesg
That's all I'm saying. You can be kind, even when you don't want to be, and maybe something good can come out of it. Like saving all of North America from Frost Giants and all of Earth from every other realm.

Squirrel Girl @unbeatablesg
Earth was saved by kindness, like, three days ago so it feels pretty relevant right now??

Squirrel Girl @unbeatablesg
OKAY! SORRY TO GET "REAL" ON "SOCIAL MEDIA," I PROMISE SQUIRREL-THEMED RETWEETS AND IDENTIFICATION OF ALL THE AMAZING SQUIRRELS IN YOUR PHOTOS WILL BEGIN AGAIN RIIIIGHT... NOW

Nancy W. @sewwiththeflo
@unbeatablsg Reading reports here of "The Leader" attacking outside the Whitney art museum, Highline entrance. Gamma-powered super-genius.

Squirrel Girl @unbeatablesg
@sewwiththeflo On it! Thanks for the heads up, concerned citizen!! I appreciate any and all CrimeTipz!!

Nancy W. @sewwiththeflo
@unbeatablsg ...Are we calling crime tips "CrimeTipz" now?

Squirrel Girl @unbeatablesg
@sewwiththeflo Uh no that was just a typo, haha, definitely not something I was trying out to see how people would react to it hahaha

Squirrel Girl @unbeatablesg
@sewwiththeflo Gotta go

Nancy W. @sewwiththeflo
@unbeatablsg Go get 'em, squirrel.

This page inspired by Bob Dylan's 1965 hit "Subterranean Homesick Blues," in which he says, "Don't follow leaders, watch the parking meters." This is good advice both for you, the reader (don't follow Hulk's gamma-irradiated villain the Leader), and also for the character depicted on this page (had he watched out for parking meters more dutifully, then he wouldn't have gotten hit by one just now).

See, because koi are fish and you could call chipmunks "chips" for short if you really wanted. Nobody does that, but you *could,* and then this nickname would be *ready.*

Mary texted to say she'll meet us at your place.
Things are going well with you two, *huh?*
Yeah, they are! They really are. It's nice.
She's this brilliant and chaotic engineer, I never know what she's gonna say next, and I never thought I'd fall in love with someone like that, but I'm really glad I did, you know?
I do. And I'm really glad too, Tomas. It's great to see you both so happy.

Nancy! Mary! Mew! We had a really successful day
Fighting crime as super heroes and
achieving our goals!!

Hey you.
Nancy, Tippy defeated a gamma-irradiated genius super villain today!
That's right! That's how *this* squirrel chooses to spend her Saturday mornings!

I saw on the news. Well done, Tips. "The Leader" brought his "Humandroids," yeah?
"Humanoids," actually.
Does that mean the name "Humandroids" is available? Because I'mma use that.

Seems to me like it'd be safer *not* to infringe on the intellectual property of a super villain, Mary.
I've said it before and I'll say it again: If super villains aren't using their intellectual property and/or doomsday devices, then they should open-source them to the rest of us.
It's the *only* way culture and/or doomsday devices progress, friends.

Nobody tell The Leader that "humanoid" actually just means "shaped like a human," and it's not scary at all! Earth media is chock-full of humanoids. You or your loved ones may already be humanoids!!

How's Doughnatello coming?
Very good, thank you. He's just been fed. I've actually been enjoying feeding my yeastie beasties twice a week, and the sourdoughs we make keep getting better.
So hey, it surprised me that Brain Drain wasn't there for that fight. A super-genius with a giant brain who builds robot bodies sounds like it'd be right up his alley.
That's a good point! I haven't heard from him for a bit. I'm gonna call him right now!
HELLO, YOU HAVE REACHED THE VOICEMAIL OF BRIAN DRAYNE, REGULAR HUMAN. SOCIETY DICTATES I MUST NOW REQUEST YOU LEAVE A MESSAGE AT "THE BEEP," AS IF VOICEMAIL WERE SOMEHOW NOVEL, SOMEHOW NOT JUST ANOTHER DREARY FACT OF MODERN LIFE, KNOWN BY ALL, TREASURED BY NONE. THIS SHARED HUMILIATION ROBS AND BELITTLES US BOTH, YET IN EXCHANGE OFFERS UP NO DEEPER MEANING, NO REDEMPTION, FOR AT ITS CORE WE FIND ONLY THE MADNESS OF CONFORMITY AND THE CHAOS OF COMPLICI--
BEEEEEP
Straight to voicemail.
That's...weird. Phone calls are normally routed right to his dome speaker. Anyone seen him the past couple of days?
Actually, no.
Come to think of it...me neither.
We were going to hang out on Friday and bury nuts, but he never showed up.
I figured he was too busy doing his usual "grappling with the essential unknowables of humanity" thing. Which on the one hand I get--being a human seems real complicated...
...but on the other hand I guess I don't get, because you never see a squirrel in the throes of existential despair??

In case you're wondering: Yes, Brain Drain's voicemail recording cut him off before he could finish saying everything he wanted.
And in case you're wondering: Yes, that was the third run he took at recording that particular message.

Huh.
...Look, it's probably nothing, but I'm gonna go stop by his regular haunts to check on him. Maybe a circuit burned out somewhere, interrupted his mobility.

I'm coming too.
We're all going. If something's happened, he could need our help.
Quick, chums! *To the usual places Brain Drain goes!*

PLATO'S DANCE CAVE
Hasn't been here since Monday.
SECURITY
Everyone here says they haven't looked on him in a while.
OZYMANDIAS STATUE PARK
NYC INDOOR POO
Staff recognized his photo and said he's missed his usu aquafit class the past few days.
We haven't seen BD since Thursday, man. You know when he's coming by?
His dunks are *poetry.*
SCHOOL OF PHILOSOPHY
APPLIED EXISTENTIALISM DEPT
...Empty.

All I know is that statue park in particular is going to last *forever*, and I am definitely *not* interested in reading any poetry that suggests otherwise!!

So Brain Drain lives in...an abandoned custodial closet in the philosophy department?
It's close to his classes, and the featureless grey walls reveal, ***and I quote,*** "essential truths that would otherwise remain obscured."
But...he should be here.
He should at least be ***somewhere.***
I don't like it. Brian's one of my top five human friends and easily my #1 brain-in-a-jar friend. I'm gonna go organize a squirrel search party, just to be safe.
Good idea.
DING
Gah. Another one.
Another what?
It's these stupid messages I've been getting.
2B
ZOOOP
There's no text, no metadata, just the same uniformly black mage for days. I think someone's script messed up, but--
That means they started around when Brian disappeared. He could be the source. Let me see.
img_0042.png
Oh my god, I should've realized--
Nope, no self-recriminations allowed. None of us knew he was missing until just now; you couldn't have known.
But there ***is*** something odd about this image...
See? Up the brightness and contrast, and it's not ***actually*** uniformly black. There's more going on here. We're gonna need a better interface than this phone.
Quick, chums! ***To the computer science lab!***

Since Brain Drain is missing we won't have the chance to show it, but you should know that one of Brain Drain's hobbies is dressing up like a bat to fight both crime ***and*** heartfelt malaise so that one day all criminals will have to grapple with...the Dark Knight of the Soul.

So let's suppose I have a robot body and I keep sending you the same non-lossy image that's clearly supposed to be a flat color but has all these pixels that are just sliiiightly off. Are you thinking what I'm thinking?
Oh snap.

Steganography.

If he's trapped somewhere--maybe his comm channels are being monitored and a picture is all he can get out--then obviously he'd--
Hey, here's a fun idea: Let's explain what steganography is for those of us who haven't taken that elective yet!
Right, sorry.
It's--well, it's spycraft, basically.

Let's say you're a spy--
Love it.
--and you want to send me a secret message but don't want it to look suspicious. So you very casually and very innocently send me a photo of your favorite animal instead: a horse.
Love that too.

Your spy trick exploits the fact that computers use a number to precisely describe the color of each and every pixel in your horse pic.
LEAST SIGNIFICANT DIGIT
MOST SIGNIFICANT DIGIT
99,999
The computer uses binary, but it's the same with regular numbers too: Digits are worth more the farther they are to the left.

Right. If I change 99,999 to 19,999, then those two numbers are 500% different, but if I change 99,999 to 99,991, that's a difference of only--what, less than one-hundredth of one percent?
Exactly. And that least significant digit, Spy Mary, is where you are going to play.
LEAST SIGNIFICANT DIGIT
99,999
19,999
99,991

Tomas, I love you, but I am honestly kinda mad you did not inform me of the possibilities of becoming Spy Mary sooner.

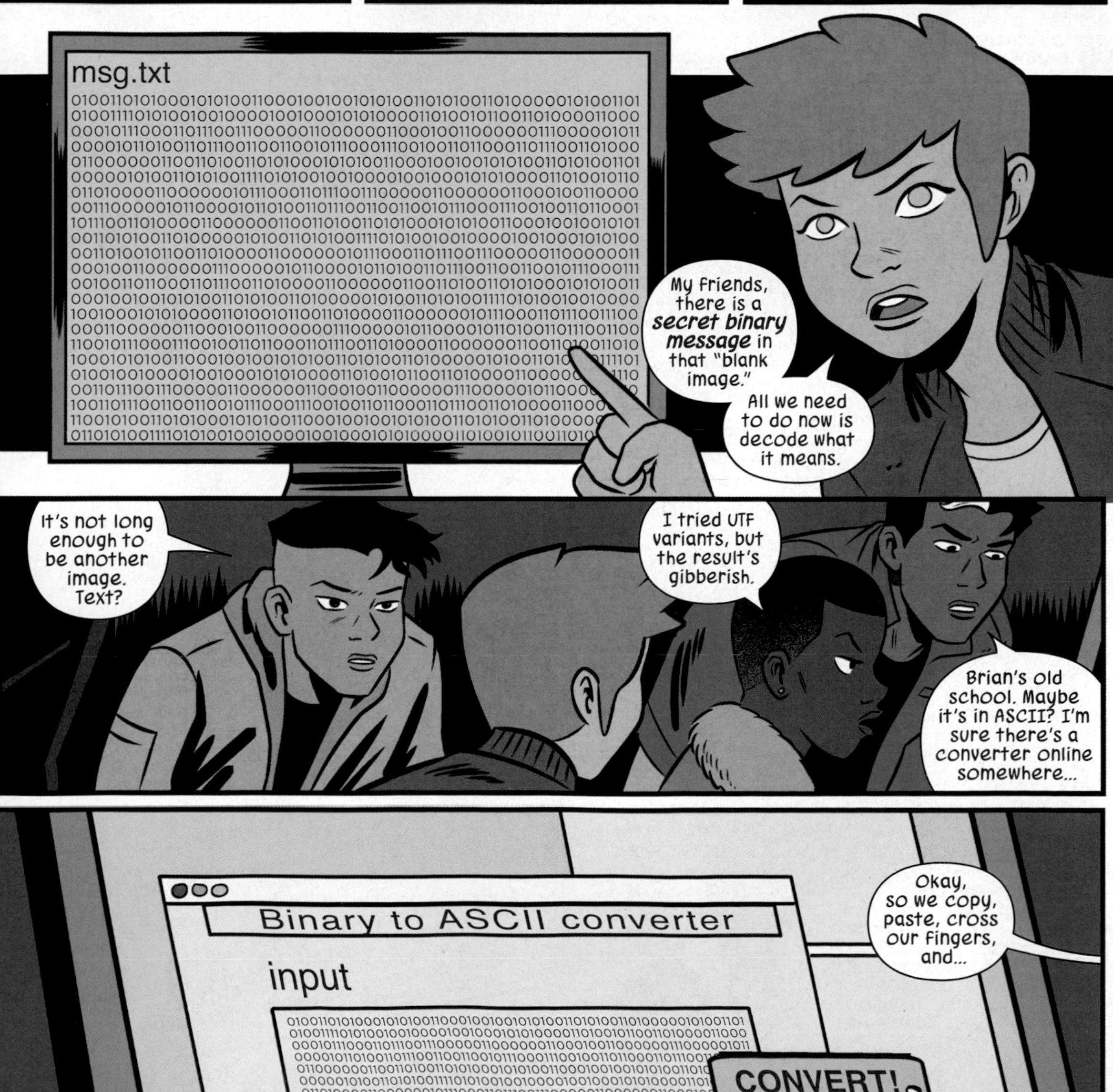

...wait for the website to load, spend a few moments wondering why it's taking so long, realize that the site's ancient CGI script is broken, go back and find a different converter, curse how realistic this comic is being right now about being online when all we really want to know is what this message actually says, repeat the same initial steps of copying and pasting, aaaaand...

Has Doreen sent in handwritten errata to Deadpool for his next edition of cards? Yes! They include "hey card #101 is in mixed case while the others are all caps," "card #1011 is repeated twice and one should clearly be card #1010," and "you forgot card #4523 for Melissa but here it is, peace out my dude."

I really wish I'd used a pseudonym when I started writing, because a) I could have some awesome name like "Chili B. Flexwell" instead of "Ryan North," and b) I'd have a secret identity that I could both protect from strangers and selectively reveal to friends. Young writers: Learn from my mistakes! Young writers: The name "Chili B. Flexwell" is available!!

He, *um*, he was making an awful lot of squirrel puns.
Yeah, I noticed. I think I'm in trouble. Nancy, can you pull up a news stream?
Already on it.

--epeating our top story: we can now confirm that the New York hero ***"Unbeatable Squirrel Girl"***--
No no no...
FACT CHANNEL LIVE

No no no no no...
--the woman who has ***single-handedly*** saved our world from the likes of Thanos and Galactus, M.O.D.O.K and Ego, Fin Fang Foom, the Mandarin, and more--
No no no no no no no...

FILE PHOTO

--is, in reality, nothing more than 20-year-old Empire State University student ***Doreen Green.***

PHOTO COURTESY DOREEN'S SOCIAL MEDIA FEED

FACT CHANNEL LIVE NEWS

Okay.
Friends, I'm having a difficult day.

It's only Melissa who could do this, she's trying to **destroy** me, she's trying to--
We've been camped outside her apartment building, where she lives with one **"Nancy Whitehead,"** but so far neither has emerged for comment. Neighbors, however, have been speaking to us. Here's a clip from earlier today.

Yeah, I didn't know 'em that well, but in retrospect she was always kinda... **secretive,** you know? **Squirrely.** Like she was **hiding** something.
NYC
NEWS

She did it. She blew up my life.
I'm so sorry, Doreen.

Maybe we can fix this. Maybe we can--
No. I appreciate it, Mary, but you can't just make people **forget** something they know. We can't--
I can't--

I'm sorry, I just--

I wasn't done being Doreen yet.

No. Nuh-uh. You get to be sad and you get to cry, but you don't get to think for one second that you're done being Doreen.
But Melissa told everyone, it's on the news, she--
And we can't change that.

But she can't change you. You're Squirrel Girl and you're Doreen, and that's just a little more public now, that's all.
You've been outed, and it sucks, but the only thing we're gonna let that mean is that now the rest of the world gets to see a bit more of the amazing person we get to see every day, okay?

Okay. Okay. Yes.
SNIF!

And, hey, at least now it might be easier when you ask for an extension on your assignments because of your extracurriculars, right?
Heh. It better be.

Okay: Gimme bright sides.

No more need to carry a change of clothes.
No more need to pretend you don't know Tippy in public.
You got mad justified motivation to rescue Brian and take down Melissa now.
Plus, at least today can't get any worse, right?
Hah!

We will remain camped outside Squirrel Girl's apartment--"compound" if you will--investigating all angles on this very shocking developmen--
BOOM
What was that?!

Get everyone back! Get back!
BOOM
Krystal, are you getting this? Get the building in frame before it--

See, *this* is why you never say, "At least things can't get any worse!" They can always get worse! Perhaps through a bad event you ironically set up with your very words!

There. *NOW* things can't get any worse.

Have those Central Park muggers learned nothing from their first encounter with Squirrel Girl?
Has all that mythological redemptive violence Doreen deployed on them somehow--*somehow*--failed to engage properly??

Swarm's backstory is that he was a mad scientist who did crazy experiments on superintelligent mutant bees, but then one day they escaped his clutches and attacked him. In that moment he faced a life-or-death choice that boiled down to whether it was nobler to transfer his consciousness to bees or not to bees. That ***was*** the question. Spoiler: He chose to be bees.

Hey there. For those of you who only know me by reputation, I'm *Melissa Morbeck*--and I'm here to talk to you today about *cooperation.*

If you're in this room, you're one of the smartest, most ambitious, and most powerful people alive. I don't presume to flatter. I presume to tell the *truth.*
Each of us operates on a level most people can only dream of: above corporations, above presidents, above governments and nations and states.

Ladies and gentlemen, each of us operates alone.
And that is our greatest *weakness.*
WHIRRR

The world has problems that can't be fixed by squabbling between the petty, transient leaders at the United Nations--an organization *by design* filled with people better at winning elections or running militaries than at actual leadership.

No, the world's problems can only be fixed from the top, with directives that *can't* be challenged. If it is to survive, the world--*our* world--needs long-term, stable, enlightened leadership.

Our world needs *us.*
And we have, thus far, *failed* it.

I would ask all readers to continue reading this comic past this page, lest someone say, "hey, Melissa makes some good points regarding the difficulty in solving problems with

Careful, woman, or I'll--

Am I wrong? Tell me, am I wrong??

The fact that we're **here** in my **underground lair** instead of up top at the head of **everything** proves I'm right. And the reason, the root cause, the nexus of failure for **everyone** here has always been the same, **each** and **every** time:

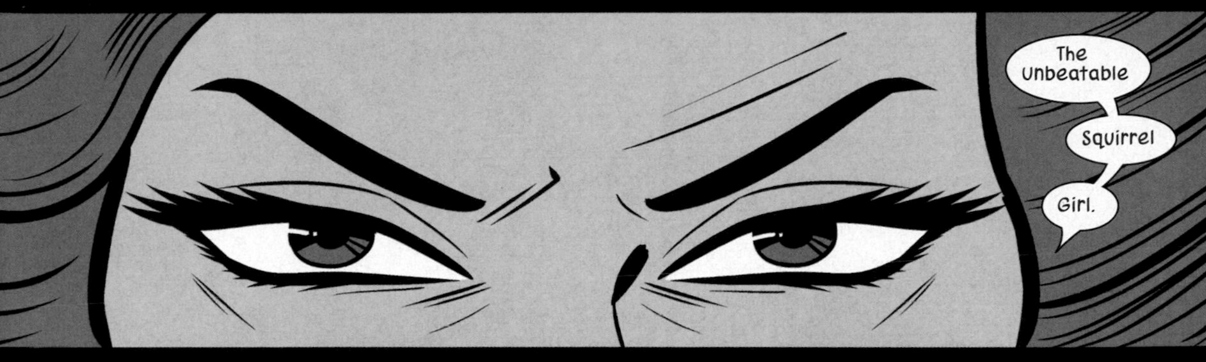

The Unbeatable
Squirrel
Girl.

In my last attempt at regime change, I could taste success--until Squirrel Girl intervened. It took a long time--too long--to recover from that, to get out of prison, to get back some of what I had.
NYPD
And everyone in this room can relate, because everyone in this room had one or more attempts stopped by this woman. This girl.

So I propose we fix that.

COMPUTER SCIENCE TRAINING
SUPER-STRENGTH
TALKS TO SQUIRRELS
PROPORTIONAL JAW STRENGTH
PREHENSILE TAIL
HEIGHTENED DURABILITY, HEALING, SPEED
KNUCKLE SPIKE
SQUIRREL AGILITY ABILITIES
Squirrel Girl has strength. We have that. She has cunning. We have that too. And anyone here can more than match her squirrel-themed powers.
And yet we still lose, because we keep ignoring, keep underestimating the one power I haven't even shown here.

"The power of friendship." Get past the twee nomenclature, and you'll see it manifesting in two ways: Squirrel Girl working with friends to defeat us, and constantly trying to transform her enemies into friends along the way.
If you're here, you're smart enough not to fall for that.

This power is what we take from her. This is how she finally loses, and we win.
We form our own union of aligned interests, stronger than hers, and thereby turn "the power of friendship" against her.

That's not even all her squirrel powers there. Melissa forgot to include "peripheral vision that's as sharp as her forward eyesight," "unparalleled tree-climbing skills," and "recently discovered ability to glow neon pink under ultraviolet light for reasons that science hasn't quiiiite figured out yet."

You all know the logistics involved in getting all of you together, so you know I'm not speaking off the cuff here. Let me preemptively address your concerns.

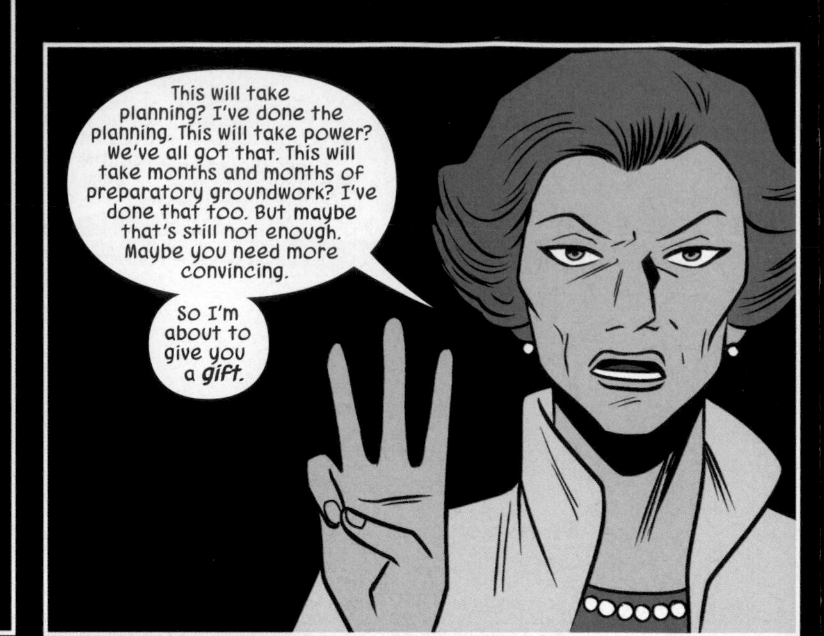

This will take planning? I've done the planning. This will take power? We've all got that. This will take months and months of preparatory groundwork? I've done that too. But maybe that's still not enough. Maybe you need more convincing.
So I'm about to give you a *gift.*

As you were all arriving here, I caused Squirrel Girl's secret identity to be revealed worldwide. Your enemy is *Doreen Green,* second-year computer science student. It's all there in your dossiers.
Squirrel Girl's secret identity is over. "Doreen Green" is over. And right now, she's *reeling.*

Just before I came on stage, I blew up her house.
I *could* tell you I'm certain the explosions got her--and I could go on to say that even *if* they didn't, her lesser enemies, emboldened by their new knowledge and her moment of public weakness, are now definitely tearing her limb from limb.

But I won't insult you. Everyone in this room is smart enough to know that's not the case.

I blew up her house because when you're an engineer you dot your I's and cross your T's, but we're all smart enough to know that Doreen Green isn't going to *die* unless we *force* her to.

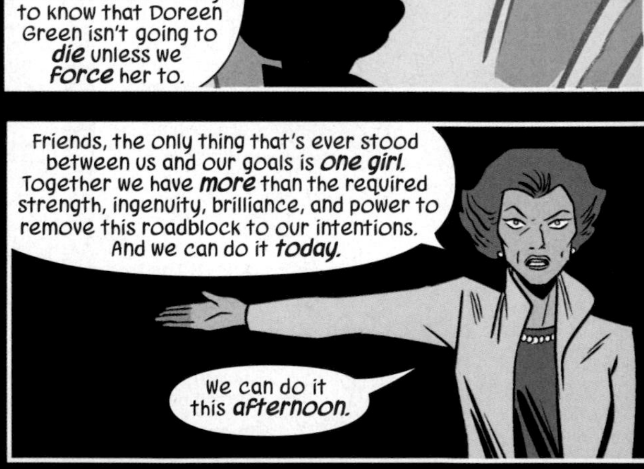

Friends, the only thing that's ever stood between us and our goals is *one girl.* Together we have *more* than the required strength, ingenuity, brilliance, and power to remove this roadblock to our intentions. And we can do it *today.*
We can do it this *afternoon.*

There's a button on your chairs: Hit *green* and you're with me. Hit red and we'll go our separate ways, no harm no foul.
This is the greatest gathering of ambitious minds the world has ever known. If we work together, right here, right now, for just *one single day,* well...

...then all we have to do is kill her.
the unbeatable Squirrel Girl

Starring:

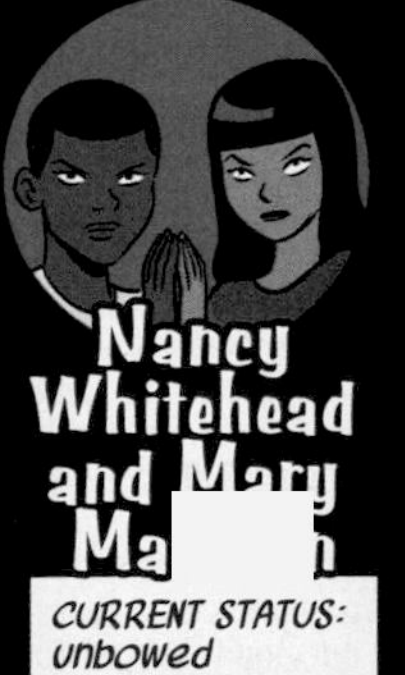
Nancy Whitehead and Mary
CURRENT STATUS: unbowed

Chipmunk Hunk and Koi Boi
CURRENT STATUS: unbroken

Squirrel Girl
CURRENT STATUS: unbeatable

Melissa Morbeck
CURRENT STATUS: unassailable

AND EVERY OTHER VILLAIN WE JUST SAW AND THEN SOME!
CURRENT STATUS: unstoppable

Letters From Nuts

Ryan!

Derek!

Send letters to mheroes@marvel.com or 135 W 50th St, 7th Floor, New York, NY 10020 (Please mark "OKAY TO PRINT")

Dear Ryan, Erica and Derek,

I've been reading and enjoying the Letters from Nuts pages in the USG collected editions for quite a while now but decided to finally write in as I heard USG was ending this year. As you probably already know, since I'm writing in, I love your comic for so many, many reasons that other people have written about countless times in the letters you've printed.

Instead of repeating those reasons, I just want you all to know that USG hands down became my favorite comic after I caught the first small text on a page on the first issue. I love to read the comics on the couch next to my fiancé and share with him the funniest moments whenever I uncontrollably laugh out loud (which happens basically once a page). We are big Brain Drain/Brian Drayne fans here.

USG has given me so many wonderful memories that I will treasure forever, a love of finding elusive Squirrel Girl merch and a beautiful comic book collection. Thank you guys for the laughs and for truly getting me into comic books for the first time. I look forward to giving these books to my child one day so he or she can enjoy them and learn there are other ways to solve conflicts than through violence and that a little bit of optimism never hurts. Also, that squirrels are awesome!

Best wishes,
Victoria S.
California

P.S. I sincerely hope I get to meet you guys one day; it's a new dream of mine! And thank you for being active on Twitter and engaging with fans (like yours truly)!

RYAN: Hey, Victoria — thank you! Letters like this are amazing to read — it's rare in life that you get people telling you that they really enjoy what you do, so thank you for that! One time my friend (Canadian) was marrying an American, and they needed letters from people who knew them both showing that their relationship was real and not an immigration scam. And I got to write one! It was really nice, talking about how I knew them both, our friendships going back years, etc. The government wanted details, so I got to write about all the things I liked best about them and all the things we'd done together and the way they'd impacted my life in this really positive way. It's not quite the same thing, but there's only a few times in life when we get to write letters like that, and thank you for writing one about us and this book.

DEREK: Thanks so much Victoria, so happy to hear all of this. I often find myself laughing out loud reading Ryan's scripts, so I know the feeling well. I also join you in being a Brain Drain fan and wanting more Squirrel Girl merch.

Dear Squirrel Girl Team,

I first found Squirrel Girl because I have been a fan of Shannon Hale for years. Reading the first SG novel felt like visiting the person I was before depression and chronic pain. There was a lot of laughter and tears. When I finished the novel I went to the library and devoured every volume of USG they had, then went to the local comic book store and bought as many back issues as I could and started my very first pull list. I gush about SG to anyone who will listen because she means the world to me. Her perseverance, problem-solving, kindness, optimism, and enthusiasm have captured my whole heart. I was incredibly saddened when I read that this chapter of her story will be coming to an end. But before it does, I wanted to thank you, everyone who puts in the work to document Doreen's adventures. Thank you for reminding me of who I am and who I want to be. Thank you for the laughs and the tears. Thank you for creating pure sunshine and hope in a world that seems darker every day. I know I will probably definitely cry when the final issue comes out.

So long, and thanks for all the ~~fish~~ kicking butts and eating nuts.

Melody
Fort Worth, Texas

RYAN: Isn't Shannon the best? Fun fact: Shannon is the best. She and her partner Dean co-wrote the Squirrel Girl novels, and here is my favorite Dean story: He is strong. REAL strong. So much so that he can easily give me a piggyback ride! I'm 2 meters tall (in nonmetric measurements, that is: hecka tall) and that makes me heavy, but Dean didn't mind and gave me my first piggyback ride in DECADES. Of course, we were on tour for the Squirrel Girl books at the time (theirs and mine!) so my first piggyback ride in DECADES was around a bookstore in front of a cheering audience. All this to say: Thank you, Melody, this was terrific to read and I'm so glad the book impacted you the way it did, and if Dean Hale ever offers you a piggyback ride, SAY YES.

DEREK: Just to back this story up, the first thing Shannon did when we met recently was show me a picture of Dean giving Ryan a piggyback ride. And, Melody, thank you! While it's sad the book is coming to an end, I think it's pretty cool that this big complete Squirrel Girl story will exist for years to come.

With news of SQUIRREL GIRL's impending end, I just wanted to thank the entire creative team on this book throughout the run. Yinz have been killing it! Everything from Squirrel Girl's Twitter engagement with the fans to the Deadpool Cards (official merchandise when???) to the fun issues like "Choose Your Own Adventure" or the zine or Norse squirrel mythology…it's just perfection.

I first heard of Squirrel Girl when a friend off-loading old comics gave me his GREAT LAKES AVENGERS run. I then proceeded to track down every single Squirrel Girl appearance/back issue. I couldn't get enough of this lovable and wacky character, and it warms my heart to see how far she's come from being this little Easter Egg Internet fan-favorite to a full-blown character with her own series, merchandise, potential TV series (fingers crossed still on that front), cartoon, Halloween costumes, doll line, etc.

So, thank you, sincerely and deeply, from a huge Squirrel Girl fan for sharing her awesomeness with the rest of the world and giving her the spotlight she has deserved all along.

Brandon "Link" Copp-Millward
Pittsburgh, PA

RYAN: Link, thank you! Also, this is my first experience with "yinz," and when I looked it up it said "Yinz is a Pittsburg equivalent to 'y'all'" and then your letter says you're from Pittsburgh. SO YOUR STORY CHECKS OUT. Thanks yinz in Pittsburgh for reading it, and I really appreciate that YOU appreciate the more experimental issues in our run! The thing I love about Squirrel Girl is that she can go anywhere: cosmic adventures in one story, street-level stuff with Kraven in the next. I'm really going to miss hanging out with her as much as I have!

DEREK: Thanks, Link! I also love the experimental issues of this run! It really shows how much you can do with this character and this universe.

DEAR SQUIRREL GIRL TEAM,

I've been reading comics for a few years now and I don't think a comic has made me laugh more, made me happy more, made me try to make everyone in my life read it more than the UNBEATABLE SQUIRREL GIRL!!! In my honest opinion, she's the most important hero in Marvel comics, and everyone else could learn a thing or two from her. I can't tell you enough how much this book means to me. Erica and Derek are the absolute perfect choices for this book, Ryan is possibly the funniest person ever, and I'm so glad it's going to reach 50 issues. (BTW, this is my first time writing in, I'm really nervous about it, but I love the team behind this book and wanted y'all to know.) I hope after this ends Ryan keeps doing more stuff for Marvel because I don't want to stop reading his stuff anytime soon.

Ellis, a 21-year-old that laughs out loud at comics in public

RYAN: Ellis, as a 38-year-old who laughs out loud at comics in public, I ENDORSE YOUR LIFESTYLE. I'd say your first letter to a comics page was a success, and thank you so much for everything — including saying I'm possibly the funniest person ever! Unfortunately this response is just sincere and not funny, so I guess I didn't live up to my reputation. THIS TIME.

DEREK: Thanks so much, Ellis. I'm a few issues ahead and can confirm there are more opportunities to laugh out loud in public coming up!

Dear UNBEATABLE Team,

When the 3-year-old in this picture saw his big sister in the Vol. 9 Letters from Nuts, he started working on his costume. Now he can be a nut too, as the Chipmunk Hunk! Luckily, he chose Tomas instead of trying to figure out how to make a credible Kraven outfit. Thanks for keeping this fun for all!

Jeffrey

RYAN: Ahhhhhh, so great! SO GREAT. And I'm glad to see Chipmunk Hunk leaning into the giant A on his shirt. I love the jacket too — with this outfit, he can definitely fight crime with chipmunk-like efficiency!!

DEREK: Perfection.

Hello Squirrel-nauts!

I wanted to thank everyone involved for the laughs and lessons over the last 58 issues, OGN, and TWO young adult novels. Squirrel Girl was first announced on my birthday, October 5, making this an extra-special series for me!

Ryan, you have inspired me with your witty writing and creative storytelling; Erica and Derek, your artwork always was top-notch; Rico, your colors popped and were spot-on! Thank you to everyone who worked on this comic!

The only question that I have is what is Doreen's birthday?

I made a drawing of what I believe are all of Squirrel Girl's outfits in her run. I hope that there will be more of Doreen and Nancy in the future!

Aaron
Brantford, Ontario

RYAN: Aaron, what a treat this picture is! Normally we get the letters for each month's issue all in a batch, but our editors sent yours as soon as it came in because they wanted to share what you'd done right away. So rad! I think your version of the snow outfit is my favorite. As for Doreen's birthday, I don't think we've ever made it explicit, but I always assumed it was when her first appearance was — which I believe puts it somewhere in December. As for more Doreen and Nancy, I hope so too. A Squirrel Girl book without Nancy would feel like — like — like some sort of hypothetical "Super" "Man" book without an equally hypothetical "Lois" "Lane"!

DEREK: Aaron, this is super cool. I love seeing all these costumes in one place. And your stylized take on Doreen is great. It's hard to pick a favorite, but I might selfishly lean toward the snow outfit as well. ;)

Dear Ryan, Derek, Rico and Erica (if you still read the letter columns),

My name is Sarah. I am a student at NYU, known as Empire State University to our good friends in the 616. I like that our New York and Marvel's New York are nearly identical except for heroes, villains, aliens, magic, and a copyright-friendly name but otherwise identical presentation of New York University (with, sometimes, Columbia University's gates, because why not?)

Unlike Doreen, however, who has a practical college major, I have inexplicably gone down the dubious path of an independent study in comic book and animation history (also a minor in animal studies, which I am frankly surprised Doreen is not pursuing).

I was hesitant to write in at first, but when I heard this series was coming to an end, I realized I wanted to say something while I had the chance. More specifically, I want to thank the makers of this book for reminding me that comics do not need to take themselves seriously to be great. I spend so much of my time trying to convince people of the legitimacy of my area of concentration — that, yes, I am actually studying comic book history and, yes, this is a field that I think warrants academic research — that I can sometimes forget why I love them in the first place: They're so limitlessly imaginative and fun.

As an Orthodox Jew, I come off as culturally bizarre. As someone on the autism spectrum, I come off as socially bizarre. One of the appealing aspects of your series is the naturalness to the quirks of your characters. Like Brain Drain, I tend to dwell in the realm of existential terror, which, for some reason, most people do not want to discuss every day at all times. Like Koi Boi, I am passionate about sharing obscure animal facts that may or may not have any pertinence in a given situation. Like Nancy, I sometimes express myself too bluntly, but I would die for my pet. And like Mary, I admire the good work of Victor Von Doom and can be something of an agent of chaos myself, as demonstrated in this sentence, which I began with the word "and" — take THAT, conventional rules of grammar! When I read the pages of UNBEATABLE SQUIRREL GIRL, and especially the footnotes underneath, I feel as though I am among friends.

You display a rich understanding of the Marvel mythos and manage to have fun with your own spin on it. The series is thoughtful but unpretentious and friendly to new readers. It includes a ridiculous cast of characters with consistently evolving personalities and great chemistry. Your rendering of the more traditional characters also feels spot-on. Your Tony Stark, for instance, keeps his loose morals and irresponsible use of technology without feeling out of place in an all-ages book. This by itself is an achievement worthy of praise, though it is also, I think, a testament to the strength of Marvel's characters that they can remain themselves in a wide array of situations and genres. Thank you for adding to this tradition of rich verisimilitude. I never thought I would enjoy a lighthearted comic as much as a gritty one, yet here I am, glad to be wrong.

I will be sad to see the end of this series. At the same time, kudos to you guys for ending on your own terms. I trust you know when you've told the story you needed to tell, and I will look out for your future projects.

I also wanted to say a special thank-you to Erica. She was the first creator I met at my very first comic con and I was too overwhelmed to utter anything articulate at the time, but she was very kind even though I did not say much beyond, "Hi, I'm Sarah. This is my first comic con and I am seriously overwhelmed." I could not have picked a better first person to meet.

So, until I pursue a degree with the potential of a lucrative career,

Make Mine Marvel

P.S. I have an internship this summer working at a wildlife rehabilitation center, which means I will be handling all sorts of animals including, yes, squirrels. By the time you read this, I will have official squirrel experience.

RYAN: Sarah, I'm so happy that through this letters page we've met so many people with Actual Squirrel Experience — and now you too! And again, thank you for this letter. It's really gratifying to hear from people whom this book has connected so well with, and I promise you that every single person involved in this book will keep making more comics real soon. So don't think of it as one book ending — think of it as multiple future books beginning, yeah? I am very jealous of your line of study; it sounds like something that would be right up my alley. Keep at it and then write some awesome books for me to read all about it, please!!

DEREK: Hi, Sarah, thanks so much for this letter. My confession is that when I started on the book, I mistakenly thought ESU was supposed to be Columbia University rather than NYU. In hindsight, it is impossibly obvious. So anyway, now parts of ESU are very fancy and that's canon.

Next:

Attention, Squirrel Scouts! Make sure to check out our production blog, **unbeatablesquirrelgirl.tumblr.com**, where we post behind-the-scenes stuff on how the book gets made, along with all sorts of cool things *you* make: fanart, cosplay, whatever!

EH!
2019

*Doreen Green doesn't just study computer science - she also studies **justice**, thanks to her being born with all the powers of a squirrel **and** all the powers of a girl! With the help of her best friends (human and squirrel), she fights crime and saves Earth on the regular. Her pals call her Doreen - which means you can too! - but if you ever see her in costume, keep her secret identity safe and call her...**The Unbeatable Squirrel Girl!***

Squirrel Girl *in a nutshell*

Squirrel Girl @unbeatablesg
Okay, my secret identity may just have been made public. But consider the source! This is MELISSA MORBECK: KNOWN BAD LADY. Remember when she tried to TAKE OVER THE WORLD?? Because I sure do

Squirrel Girl @unbeatablesg
and YES she's a brilliant engineer and YES she's the one who taught us all about the iron rings all the engineers in Canada wear to remind them of their responsibilities every time they sign off on a blueprint and YES she's incredibly clever and brilliant --

Squirrel Girl @unbeatablesg
-- hold on this tweet thread isn't going the way i intended --

Squirrel Girl @unbeatablesg
The POINT is that she's MANIPULATIVE and thinks she's better than the rest of us and thinks that she's somehow qualified to control the world! Is THAT someone you want to be listening to? Even if they are sharing TRUE FACTS vis-à-vis my identity??

Squirrel Girl @unbeatablesg
Anyway, yes. My name is Doreen Green, and I'm the Unbeatable Squirrel Girl. This used to be a fact only a few trusted loved ones knew, and now everyone knows it, so CONGRATS, YOU NOW KNOW A COOL FACT, ENJOY

Squirrel Girl @unbeatablesg
And normally I'd be MORE than happy to hang out here and answer everyone's questions, but my friend BRAIN DRAIN is missing, so if anyone has seen him please reply to this thread to let me know!!

Squirrel Girl @unbeatablesg
He's easy to recognize, he's a brain in a jar in a robot body and he's REAL good at nihilism, which is how you can tell him apart from all those other brains in jars on robot bodies that are slightly less good at the ol' nihilism

Squirrel Girl @unbeatablesg
UPDATE: some of y'all have decided to crash my CS lab in order to fight me??

Squirrel Girl @unbeatablesg
UPDATE: SOME OF Y'ALL ARE SUPER VILLAINS I'VE DEFEATED IN THE PAST AND WHO ARE CARRYING A GRUDGE YOU'D NOW LIKE TO SETTLE ONCE AND FOR ALL???

Squirrel Girl @unbeatablesg
UPDATE: SOME OF Y'ALL ARE CURRENTLY PUNCHING ME AS I'M TRYING TO SHARE MY CONTENT ONLINE??

Squirrel Girl @unbeatablesg
UPDATE: I GOTTA GO DEAL WITH THIS, MORE SOON, ALSO I KNOW YOU'RE LIVESTREAMING THIS @EPICCRIMEZ AND IT'S SO STUPID SO PLEASE STOP

Epic Crimez @epiccrimez
@unbeatablesg never

Squirrel Girl @unbeatablesg
@epiccrimez these crimez barely even rise to the level of epic fyi

search! 

- #doreengreenissquirrelgirl
- #squirrelgirlisdoreengreen
- #trashtalkwithcomplimentsinit
- #ironmanunderoos
- #deadpoolcards

Good. I'm glad you're all on board. Squirrel Girl has handed each of us our greatest defeats, and with her out of the way, I'm sure you'll *all* agree *nothing* can stop u--
Careful, Ms. Morbeck...

...for you are *perilously* close to daring to speak for *Doom.*

I will now explain the terms of my participation--once. Know that I do not take orders from lesser people, which is the same as saying I do not take orders from *anyone.*
Know also there is not a universe in which I am stupid enough to believe this team will stay intact after Squirrel Girl is dead.

One of two things is about to happen: Either you will all foolishly *perish* trying to defeat Doreen--in which case, none of you shall irk me again and Doom will triumph...
...or you will *succeed,* and Doreen Green, the single greatest threat to my machinations, will be eliminated. If so, *again* Doom triumphs.

Whether through luck or fate, this plan--though it did not spring from the brilliant mind of Doom--meets with my approval *prima facie,* for one reason: It acknowledges, accepts, and bends itself toward the one universal truth, the only eternal and unalterable fact of the universe...

...No matter what happens, Doom *always* triumphs.

Of course Doctor Doom drops Latin phrases into his speech to both show off his education and intimidate other people. He's *Doctor Doom.*

Naturally. I would expect nothing less, Doctor. I've been planning for the same eventualities that you have, and once Doreen Green is gone...
...may the best tactician win.
Yes. That is the same as saying "may Doom win," which is the correct wish.

But until then, I welcome your help. I welcome *all* your help. And as proof of that, I'd like to give you one last welcoming gift, something beyond Doreen's secret identity.
It's another ace up my sleeve, and the beginning of our shared plan...
Brain Drain, would you step out on stage please?
VRRT
VRRT
VRRRRRRT

In case you're wondering, *yes,* Whiplash is well aware that he's out of his league and clearly only been invited to this meeting because The Abomination was unavailable, and *yes,* he's going to do his level best to make a good impression on all these evil geniuses!

Meanwhile, back at the CS lab...
Stop it! Every one of you lab invaders is acting like an idiot!
That's funny, because you're acting like someone who's about to be stung to death by bees in just a few more seconds!
Hey, let's see who drops first, shall we?
KLIK

I just want you to hear what I'm saying! If you'll just calm down for a second and liste--
PLONK
Come on, man.

Surprised to see me again, Doreen? The Boomerang always comes back, baby!!
Hey, can I borrow one of those?
Get your own, loser.

Eugh. Fine. We do it the hard way.

OPEN!

Now you're all gonna stand down or I'm gonna pull this alarm and let the ceiling sprinklers do their thing.
And I seem to recall something about bees being unable to fly when they're wet?

That line The Boomerang used is pretty obvious, but he still uses it every chance he gets. Why? Well, he used to have some other zingers, but he forgot them. It's okay: He's sure they'll come back to him eventually.

You may have defeated me with water *last* time,* but my associates here don't share that weakness.
*EDITOR'S NOTE: It happened in THE UNBEATABLE SQUIRREL GIRL #7-- or at least, there's a possibility it did! It'll make sense when you read the issue, honest.
Sure, but you've all got a *different* weakness now. Care to hear what it is?
Sure!

None of you are *thinking* about what you're doing!

You find out *Doreen Green* has a secret identity, and the first thing you do is come here to *attack her?* Hello?! I'm the *last* person on Earth you should be attacking!
I'm a civilian with super-powers who's suddenly free to use them, which means I can now defend myself better than any other civilian on the planet!

And let's say you decide to go ahead with this anyway. What, you think attacking me on my worst day is going to make me *not* want to fight back?
You think my secret identity leaking *hasn't* given me tons of motivation to beat you guys *for real,* so that *anyone* who even *thinks* about coming after me down the road will remember what happened to *you* and get warned off *forever?*

In what universe is this *smart,* fellas? In what universe are you *ever* gonna come out on top here?
Uh...

...he started it?

Blockchain's criminal record is growing all the time, and it's stored publicly in a distributed ledger.

For example, he can produce hundreds of acorns filled with nutrition for squirrels while also shooting lasers out of his eyes. Good combo. Solid dude all around in my opinion.

A few big leaps later...
I'm glad I didn't have to destroy a whole lab's worth of university computer equipment to stop a bunch of bees possessed by a mad scientist.
I'm certain that sentence has never been said before in history until now, and *I'm* glad I was here to witness it.
Should only be one more leap until we arrive at the apartment, Nancy. I'm sure Mew's safe.
Thanks, Doreen.
It occurs to me that with Doreen's identity being made public, it won't take much to figure out that Tomas Lara-Perez is Chipmunk Hunk or that Ken Shiga is Koi Boi.
True.
But that's already information Melissa knows too, so it's probably best to assume she's going to leak it, if she hasn't already.
Yeah. No matter what happens next...
LEAP
LEAP
FLOPP
...we're all in this together.

Koi Boi's core muscles are *insane.* Also, since we're running out of time to establish this: Koi Boi also has some magnetic-sensitive cells, like fish do, which gives him an innate sense of direction while navigating Earth's magnetic field. Just a nice perk. Enjoy, Ken!

The media left?
It seems they were drawn off by reports and photos of you *very* publicly and dramatically fighting a bee man on campus. Anonymously submitted. By me, several minutes ago.
Owe you one, Mary.
Mew?

Squirrel Scouts noticed the explosives after you left. We managed to get everyone out in time but didn't know how to disarm the bombs themselves.
Because the bomb had red wires and green wires and squirrels are red-green color-blind?
You know it!
PRRRRRRR...
I can't thank you enough, Tippy. You did *great.* Every squirrel here did great.
It was amazing! We chased the humans out of there with our *teeth.* I tell you, Doreen, you ever need a building evacuated again, you just let me know. I'm little but I'm real strong!
You absolutely are, Archie. Thank you.
Also I've got fleas so now some of the humans have fleas too, haha.
I'm gonna get you a special cream later, little dude.
Sweet I love special creams

It's true: Squirrels can distinguish red and green from other colors, but not from each other. We didn't know this until a study in 1987 discovered it! Squirrel science is always advancing!!

We tried to warn you, but the ESU computer lab is brand-new and doesn't have any windows in it, so it was taking us some time to chew our way in.
You would've made it in eventually.
Literally no doubt in my mind.
BUMP

So! I don't know about you all, but Melissa kidnapping my friend and blowing up my life and my house and almost blowing up my co-parented cat makes me feel like giving her a piece of my mind. Friends...

...let's go to Central Park and finish this, shall we??

I don't think we should bring Mew there though. Melissa is literally a super villain.
Right. Thank you. Good thinking.
Friends...

...let's leave Mew with the neighbors across the street who have always been really kind to us and then go to Central Park and finish this, shall we??
Hello

Archie from the previous page is one of several squirrels in this book based on real-life squirrels me and my friends know! Specifically, Archie and my friend Trin met earlier this year when she found him incapacitated on a street and brought him to a wildlife rehab center, where he was treated and then released! And now he's comic book famous. Good job, Archie!!

That statue is real, but you're not allowed to climb on it in real life! You're not allowed to climb on it in this comic either! ***Melissa what are you doing??***

Ooh, I'm quaking in my furry boots, Melissa. What is it this time? More lions? Bears? **Mosquitoes??** Because with or without a secret identity, I've already beaten you **once** and I can do it aga--
SWOOO

SWOOSH
Hey Doreen.

Tony!!
Heard your identity got publicized. Been there, done that. Mine was under different circumstances, but still.
Rough times.

Figured I'd come by and lend a hand. After all-- that's what friends are for, right?

But there's something else that friends are for too. What was it again...?
Oh right, I remember now.

PWEEEE

Having each other's backs.
SHOOOM

And wouldn't you know it--that was the only warning shot I loaded into the suit this morning.
Guess you'd better come quietly, Melissa.
Looks like I've got backup, Melissa!
Yeah, Melissa!
Yeah!!

Oh Tony. Constant, reliable Tony.
Fail to see how that's a bad thing, Mel.
Oh, it's not. It's a great thing.
One can always trust in the arrogance of Tony Stark.

The smartest man in the room, and the only one *stupid* enough to say it out loud every single chance he gets.
The man with such *supreme* confidence in his own tech that he'd never even *think* to check if a message he got via his AI helpers--say, one telling him that Squirrel Girl was in Central Park and needed assistance...

...actually originated from *outside* his own network.
Okay--fair point, but I fail to see how luring me here helps anyone but the good guys. Who are *US*, by the way.
And why would you? You fail to see *everything*, Tony.

You failed to see when an employee on your compiler team started buying houses that should've been *well* beyond his pay grade.
You failed to see when that updated compiler started adding backdoors to every piece of code it touched, including yours, invisible even to a code review.

And you *certainly* failed to see when every line of Stark source code was fed through that same compiler for *months.*
Shut up. *Melissa.* You didn't.
Oh girl, I most definitely did.

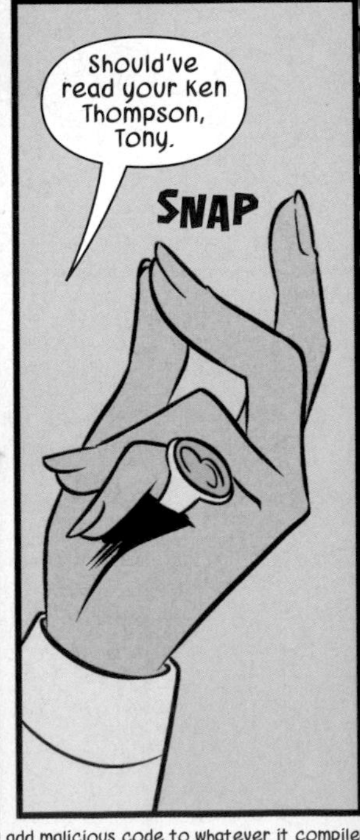

Should've read your Ken Thompson, Tony.
SNAP

Melissa's referring to a famous paper called "Reflections on Trusting Trust" that shows how a compiler can be altered to secretly add malicious code to whatever it compile Then you can use that compiler to compile *itself*, thereby hiding all evidence of your shenanigans! This is advanced computer science, so it makes sense these genius enginee would reference it, therefore changing Melissa's last line here from "weird and confusing" to "really really excellent character writing, wow, good work Ryan"!

Tony Stark not expecting to leave the house today--and therefore deciding that today is a Pants Are Optional Day--is the most relatable Tony Stark has ever been.

Just in case you thought it'd be fun to do this, don't waste your time! It's not fun at all! It hurts, and the fact that I have so much time to discuss the experience in detail while being knocked through the air shows how unpleasant and powerful these blasts really arrrreeeeeee!

Doreen! Are you okay?!
Eugh.
Kinda wish you'd loaded a few more warning shots into the suit this morning, Tony.

I'll add that to my "Tony's List of Things He Really Wishes He'd Done Differently Today."
Hey. I appreciate that, pard.

That's one shot down, Tony. Let's see how many more she can take until she gives out, huh?
I won't let you hurt him, Iron Ring. I won't let you hurt anyone.

Did you miss the part where I said my goal here today was to kill you?
Whether Tony takes the shot or you do, either way I'm coming out on top here!
PWEEE
I don't think so.
Because Doreen isn't taking the next hit.

We are.
And it'll be the last shot you ever fire at anyone.
That's right. He's my boyfriend.

On Mary's old dating profile, her "things my ideal partner does" section included the standard things we all put, like "engineering," "mad science," and "regular science too I guess"--but right there at the top was "defiantly threatening a super villain on my or a friend's behalf."

Ken. Tomas. I wondered when you'd grow your spines. Now, what was the reaction you were looking for here?
Oh, right.

Oh no, I'm so scared! A naked man and some CS undergrads--only a handful of whom actually have powers--are here to stop me! Whatever will I do??
Make fun all you want, Iron Ring, but you're still just *one woman* in a *stolen suit.*

Ah, that's true. It *would* be great if I had some powerful friends in my corner, especially if they all shared the same goal and were willing to work *together* to achieve it.
CHOOOM
I should really get on that.

Because I think you of all people, Doreen, know how truly *unbeatable* that can make someone.

TO SUPER VILLAINS
VICTOR "DOCTOR" VON DOOM
- THIS LATVERIAN KING, DIPLOMAT, INVENTOR, AND MARTIAL ARTIST ALSO HAS A BRILLIANT INTELLECT, AN INDOMITABLE WILL, AND UNPARALLELED SKILLS IN THE DARK ARTS!
- HE ALSO PAINTS AND PLAYS PIANO, LADIES
- HE'S OBSESSED WITH DESTROYING REED RICHARDS
- WEAKNESSES: NONE :(
- SKILLS: UM, EVERY SKILL, BASICALLY??
- HE'S EXTREMELY DANGEROUS AND COULD EASILY LEVEL ENTIRE CITIES IF HE GETS MAD
- FUN FACT: HE DIDN'T ACTUALLY EARN HIS PhD! HE'S A FAKE DOCTOR!! YOU SHOULD TELL HIM THAT, I BET IT'LL GO GREAT FOR YOU
YOU KNOW HOW SOME PEOPLE HAVE EGOS THE SIZE OF PLANETS? WELL DOOM'S EGO IS SO BIG, IT MAKES EGO THE LIVING PLANET FEEL INADEQUATE!! ZING!
CARD 66 OF 4522
THE LEADER
- OKAY SO YOU KNOW HOW BRUCE BANNER GOT BLASTED BY GAMMA RAYS AND NOW WHEN HE'S ANGRY HE GETS STRONG? WELL SAM STERNS GOT BLASTED BY GAMMA RAYS AND NOW WHEN HE'S ANGRY HE GETS REAL SMART! AND THAT'S HIS SECRET, CAP: HE'S ALWAYS ANGRY
- HE'S GOT LOTS OF SMARTS IN THE "GENETICS," "PHYSICS," AND "ROBOTICS" DEPARTMENTS, IS FULLY CAPABLE OF MASTERING ANY SUBJECT, AND HAS PERFECT RECALL--BUT IS HE SMART ENOUGH TO UNDERSTAND THE HUMAN EMOTION OF... LOVE?
- I'M GETTING WORD THAT HE IS EASILY SMART ENOUGH TO FULLY UNDERSTAND LOVE, AND ALSO THAT LOVE REALLY ISN'T ALL THAT COMPLICATED FOR MOST PEOPLE. WELL, GREAT. JUST GREAT
SO WHAT IF I FIND MY FEELINGS AND THE EMOTIONS OF OTHERS CONFUSING?! I'M WORKING ON IT AND WE ALL FACE OUR OWN CHALLENGES IN LIFE!!
CARD 386 OF 4522
BARON MORDO
- OKAY THIS TRANSYLVANIAN NOBLEMAN LEARNED SORCERY FROM THE SAME TEACHER WHO TAUGHT DOCTOR STRANGE, BUT MORDO PLANNED TO KILL HIS TEACHER INSTEAD! RUDE
- IMAGINE "DOCTOR STRANGE BUT BAD" AND YOU'VE GOT THIS GUY: LOTS OF SKILLS IN THE BLACK ARTS, HE CAN KILL YOU WITH MAGIC BLASTS FROM HIS HANDS, SUMMON DEMONS, THAT SORT OF THING
- THE DEMONS ARE KINDA FUN TO PARTY WITH, BUT WITH MORDO AS THE PRICE OF ADMISSION: NO THANKS!!
MORE LIKE BARON BORE-DO! ...IS WHAT I'D BE SAYING IF I WASN'T CERTAIN HE WOULD KILL ME WITH MAGIC THE SECOND HE HEARD ME SAYING IT!
DEADPOOL'S GUIDE TO SUPER VILLAINS
CARD 747 OF 4522
M.O.D.O.K.
- M.O.D.O.K. STANDS FOR "MECHANICAL ORGANISM DESIGNED ONLY FOR KISSING"! HE'S A WORLD-CLASS SMOOCHER WHO--
- WAIT, NO, SORRY, I'M JUST GETTING WORD THAT I WAS THINKING OF THE WRONG GUY. THIS ONE IS DESIGNED ONLY FOR KILLING. NO IDEA WHAT HIS SMOOCHING IS LIKE BUT PROBABLY NOT GREAT SO DON'T WASTE YOUR TIME
- M.O.D.O.K. IS A GUY WHO UNDERWENT AN EXPERIMENTAL PROCEDURE TO MAKE HIM SMARTER, AND IT WORKED BUT ALSO MADE HIM EVIL! HIS GIANT HEAD HOLDS AN EQUALLY GIANT BRAIN
- HE HAS A HOVERCHAIR (PRETTY COOL) AND IS SO SMART HE ALMOST KNOWS WHAT YOU'RE GONNA DO BEFORE YOU DO IT AND CAN MENTALLY GENERATE FORCE FIELDS (ALSO COOL, NOT GONNA LIE)
MO' DOK, MO' PROBLEMS! THAT'S WHAT I SAY WHENEVER I SEE THIS GUY! BUT HE NEVER LAUGHS AT IT?!
DEADPOOL'S GUIDE TO SUPER VILLAINS
DORMAMMU
- THIS DEMON'S NICKNAMES INCLUDE "THE DREAD ONE," "THE EATER OF SOULS," AND "THE LORD OF CHAOS AND DARKNESS." SO IF YOU'RE THINKING OF THE GUY WHO LIVES IN UNIVERSITY HOUSING, THAT'S "DORM AMMU," AND YOU WANT CARD #2512 INSTEAD
- THIS ANCIENT BEING IS THE MOST POWERFUL AND HATEFUL OF ALL AND HE DREAMS OF ENSLAVING EVERYONE! HE LIVES IN HIS OWN DIMENSION OF HORROR, SO IF YOU THINK YOUR GUY MIGHT LIVE IN STUDENT HOUSING, I CANNOT STRESS ENOUGH THE VALUE OF CHECKING OUT CARD #2512 BEFORE FREAKING OUT ALL THE WAY
AS LONG AS DOCTOR STRANGE REMAINS SORCERER SUPREME, OUR UNIVERSE HAS AT LEAST A TEENY-WEENIE HOPE OF NOT BEING CONSUMED BY HIS FIERY GRASP! SO THAT'S NICE!!
DEADPOOL'S GUIDE TO SUPER VILLAINS
CARD 660 OF 4522
TASKMASTER
- THIS DUDE CAN "MASTER" ANY "TASK" JUST BY SEEING IT PERFORMED! OH THAT'S WHERE HIS NAME COMES FROM, HA HA I JUST REALIZED THAT. COOL
- IT'S SERIOUSLY CRAZY THOUGH, HE JUST HAS TO SEE SOMETHING AND HE CAN DO IT PERFECTLY! LIKE IF HE SEES AN OLYMPIC ATHLETE RAMP HER BIKE OFF A SWEET JUMP HE CAN INSTANTLY RAMP HIS OWN BIKE OFF A SWEET JUMP EXACTLY AS WELL!!
- ANYWAY GUESS WHAT, THIS DUDE IS GREAT AT EVERYTHING AND YOU CAN'T BEAT HIM IN A FIGHT BECAUSE HE CAN INSTANTLY MASTER YOUR OWN SKILLS AND THEN USE THEM AGAINST YOU.
THIS GUY CAN MASTER SOME FRIGGIN' TASKS, I'LL TELL YOU WHAT!
DEADPOOL'S GUIDE TO SUPER VILLAINS
CARD 81 OF 4522
FIN FANG FOOM
- AN ALIEN FROM SPACE THAT LOOKS LIKE A DRAGON! AMAZING. I LOVE THIS GUY??
- HE CAN FLY, SPIT COMBUSTIBLE ACID FROM HIS MOUTH, PLUS HE AGES REAL SLOWLY AND HE'S SUPER STRONG. HE CAN ALSO SHAPE-SHIFT AND TALK TELEPATHICALLY! I WOULD LOVE TO TALK TELEPATHICALLY, NOBODY WOULD EVER BE ABLE TO GET ME TO SHUT UP EVER AGAIN, IT'S ALL I WANT OUT OF LIFE
- ANYWAY HE CAME HERE TO INVADE EARTH AND THEN HIBERNATED FOR HUNDREDS OF YEARS BEFORE WAKING UP, SO PLEASE DON'T LET HIM TAKE IT OVER UNTIL I'M DONE WITH IT, THANKS
WHERE DOES HE GET HIS LITTLE SHORTS MADE? AND WHY?
DEADPOOL'S GUIDE TO SUPER VILLAINS
CARD 4010 OF 4522
WHIPLASH
- ANTON VANKO IS OBSESSED WITH REVENGING HIMSELF AGAINST THOSE HE BELIEVES HAVE WRONGED HIM! SO IF YOU'VE EVER WRONGED HIM IN THE PAST BEFORE READING THIS CARD, SURPRISE, YOU'VE GOT AN ARCH-NEMESIS NOW! EVEN IF YOU DON'T KNOW IT
- ANTON STOLE A PIECE OF AN IRON MAN SUIT AND USED IT TO REVERSE ENGINEER HIS OWN ARMOR, ONLY HIS HAS ENERGY WHIPS INSTEAD, WHICH IS... WELL, LOOK, IT'S A CHOICE. IT'S DEFINITELY A CHOICE, AND ANTON HAS MADE IT.
- THOSE WHIPS CAN CUT THROUGH FLESH LIKE A KNIFE CUTS THROUGH BUTTER, WHICH IS TO SAY: REASONABLY WELL. HONESTLY IF THE BUTTER IS COLD I ALWAYS KINDA STRUGGLE WITH BOTH CUTTING AND SPREADING IT AND IT ALWAYS ENDS UP JUST SMUSHING INTO MY TOAST
- AND YES I'VE TRIED MICROWAVING THE BUTTER TO SOFTEN IT BUT YOU'VE GOT, WHAT, 0.00002 SECONDS BETWEEN "BUTTER TOO HARD" AND "BUTTER INSTANTLY MELTED"? COME ON, BUTTER, I JUST WANT SOME NICE TOAST HERE
- THIS IS WHY I PREFER MARGARINE: IT'S A MUCH MORE SPREADABLE BUTTER SUBSTITUTE AT FRIDGE TEMPERATURE
I MAY HAVE GOTTEN SLIGHTLY OFF TOPIC? ANYWAY! ENJOY YOUR NEW ARCH-NEMESIS WHO HATES YOU FOREVER NOW! HE GETS MURDEROUS ON PURPOSE!

PEOPLE: "What I like about *Squirrel Girl* is that it's such a dense read--you really get your money's worth!"
ME: "Sweet, here's an insane amount of Deadpool cards all filled with text crammed onto a single page!!"
PEOPLE: "*Hmm* on second thought what I really love about other comics is that they're actually such a reasonable and quick read"

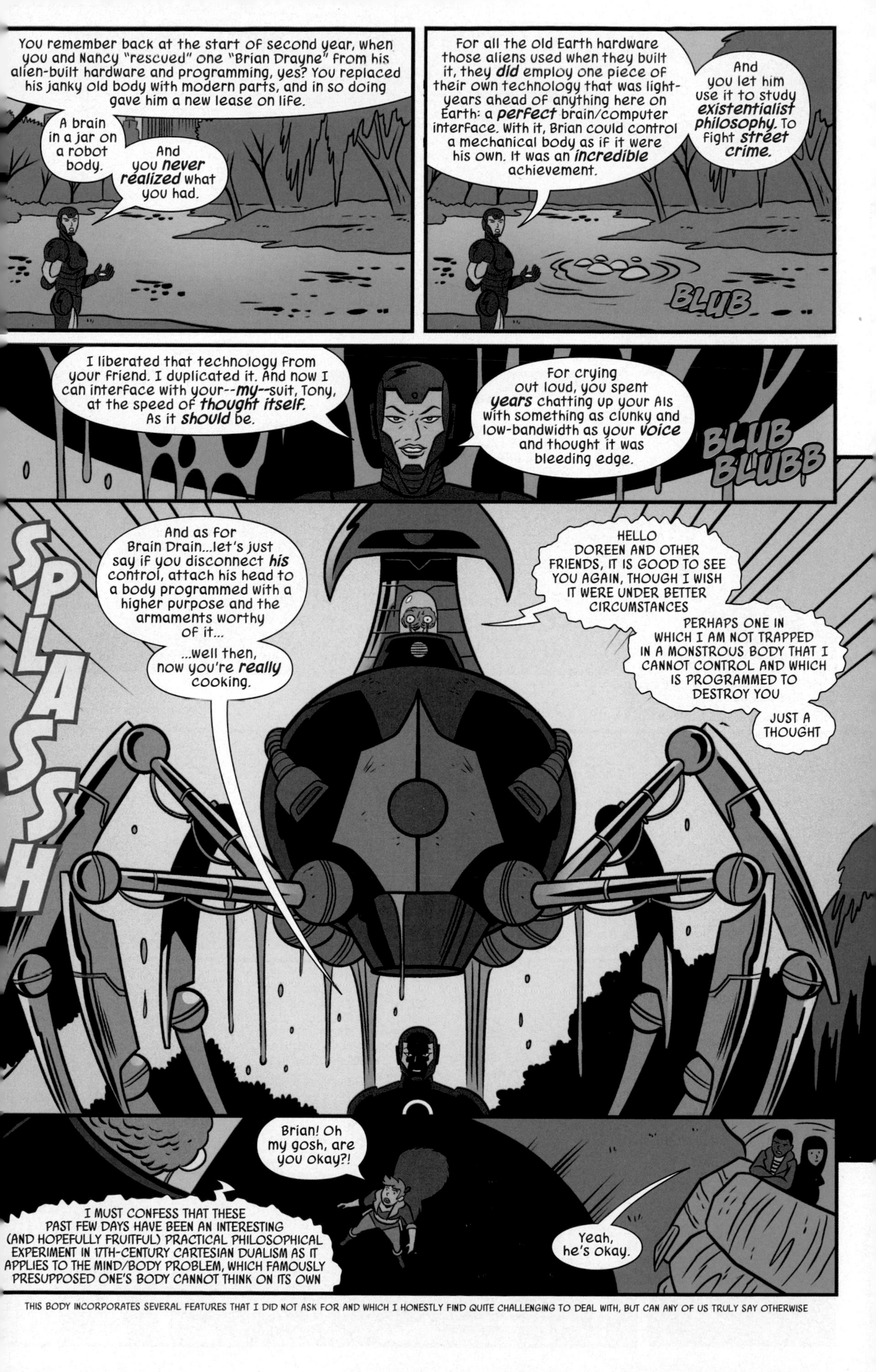

You remember back at the start of second year, when you and Nancy "rescued" one "Brian Drayne" from his alien-built hardware and programming, yes? You replaced his janky old body with modern parts, and in so doing gave him a new lease on life.
A brain in a jar on a robot body.
And you never realized what you had.
For all the old Earth hardware those aliens used when they built it, they did employ one piece of their own technology that was light-years ahead of anything here on Earth: a perfect brain/computer interface. With it, Brian could control a mechanical body as if it were his own. It was an incredible achievement.
And you let him use it to study existentialist philosophy. To fight street crime.
BLUB
I liberated that technology from your friend. I duplicated it. And now I can interface with your--my--suit, Tony, at the speed of thought itself. As it should be.
For crying out loud, you spent years chatting up your AIs with something as clunky and low-bandwidth as your voice and thought it was bleeding edge.
BLUB BLUBB
SPLASSH
And as for Brain Drain...let's just say if you disconnect his control, attach his head to a body programmed with a higher purpose and the armaments worthy of it...
...well then, now you're really cooking.
HELLO DOREEN AND OTHER FRIENDS, IT IS GOOD TO SEE YOU AGAIN, THOUGH I WISH IT WERE UNDER BETTER CIRCUMSTANCES
PERHAPS ONE IN WHICH I AM NOT TRAPPED IN A MONSTROUS BODY THAT I CANNOT CONTROL AND WHICH IS PROGRAMMED TO DESTROY YOU
JUST A THOUGHT
Brian! Oh my gosh, are you okay?!
I MUST CONFESS THAT THESE PAST FEW DAYS HAVE BEEN AN INTERESTING (AND HOPEFULLY FRUITFUL) PRACTICAL PHILOSOPHICAL EXPERIMENT IN 17TH-CENTURY CARTESIAN DUALISM AS IT APPLIES TO THE MIND/BODY PROBLEM, WHICH FAMOUSLY PRESUPPOSED ONE'S BODY CANNOT THINK ON ITS OWN
Yeah, he's okay.
THIS BODY INCORPORATES SEVERAL FEATURES THAT I DID NOT ASK FOR AND WHICH I HONESTLY FIND QUITE CHALLENGING TO DEAL WITH, BUT CAN ANY OF US TRULY SAY OTHERWISE

HEY DID YOU GET MY MESSAGE
We did! We're here to save you, Brian!
THANKS I VERY MUCH LOOK FORWARD TO THAT
Ah yes, the "hidden message" I allowed him to send.
MELISSA I CANNOT TELL IF THAT IS TRUE OR MERE BRAVADO COVERING FOR AN OVERSIGHT
HEARING WHAT WAS BEING SAID ON LAND JUST NOW WAS DIFFICULT ON ACCOUNT OF HOW I WAS HIDING IN A LAKE
So let's see--people lured onto my turf: check. New suit: check. Scorpion tank robot body: check. Unstoppable team of allies: check. If I'm not mistaken, that's all I need to kill you??
Wait! Um-- before you attack, you should know that, uh...
That what? That I should delay just a little bit longer, because the second your suit flew off in the field, the Avengers were automatically notified and are certainly on their way to rescue you as we speak?

First thing my compiler did was comment out that little line of code, Tony. Nobody else is coming.
I really don't like you, Melissa.
Not sure how that's my problem, Tony.
So! The only thing standing between us and victory is Squirrel Girl, and all she's got, friends, is a man too arrogant for pants and some animal-themed pals who haven't even graduated yet.
I don't know about you...

...but I *like* those odds.

Letters From Nuts

Ryan!

Derek!

Send letters to mheroes@marvel.com or 135 W 50th St, 7th Floor, New York, NY 10020 (Please mark "OKAY TO PRINT

Hey, nutbutts! I finally found out how to send an email, so I can write a letter to you now! If it weren't for walking around a comic book store in boredom, I would never have discovered Squirrel Girl. I was going by a shelf, and BOOM, there's a girl with a big fluffy tail about to punch a big squirrel with a horn in the face! I had no idea my favorite yard animal had a Marvel super hero counterpart... Speaking of yard animals, my woodpile is home to my very own Tippy-Toe. His name is Peanut and he's really cute.

To answer that message in issue #46, yes, we need a "Felicitations...to the sister! I am WHALE!" shirt right now. I will wear it every day of my life.

Butt slapping me now, friends,
Gillian

RYAN: Gillian, you are going to be thrilled when you go back and read some previous arcs, because there MAY be one not just with squirrels, but with a character sharing YOUR VERY NAME. I promise this is real and not just a scam to hand-sell single copies of back issues through the letter column! Though it WOULD be the perfect scheme...

Say hi to Peanut for me! I'm sorry we don't have an official shirt for you to wear...yet??

DEREK: Thanks, Gillian! Put me on the list for wanting an official Rachel-whale shirt too, please (I can wear a shirt with my own art on it, right?).

Dear Squirrel Girl FUNUTics,

Wow. As if your consistency in putting out the best comic every month weren't enough, y'all continue to impress. From that very first panel on page 7 of USG #45, the snowy woods sequence captured my attention and my heart. Derek's pulled off some amazing sequences before—the kart racing pages in *Jughead* remain some of the most fun images I've ever seen in a comic—but the snowy woods sequence goes beyond fun to outright beautiful (shout-out to Rico for the perfect coloring of sky and snow). These images have helped me to better appreciate a classic poem; I "get it" in a deeper way now.

And, of course, Doreen continues to impress. Such a healthy expression of anger in breaking up the teams with Rachel. Such a sense of hope—whereas the average super hero is probably a Kierkegaardian Knight of Infinite Resignation (or even just a unique sort of Aesthete), Doreen might be an honest-to-goodness Knight of Faith. And when she's tired and in need of inspiration, she turns to nature and poetry? We already knew she was special, but the layers of specialness go so deep. Thanks to the whole team for this incredible series. Also, I know there are only a few issues left, but more Rachel, please. She's definitely the breakout Asgardian god/investigative journalist of 2019.

Peace,
Craig E. Bacon
Irmo, SC

RYAN: Craig, thank you! This means a lot to me, because I was so happy and oddly proud that we could, in the middle of a fate-of-the-universe, company-wide crossover, have a break in the middle of the issue for three pages of poetry, and it made perfect sense. Doreen is a really special lady, and I'm going to miss her a lot!! The sequence wouldn't have worked at all without Derek and Rico (and our letterer Travis) bringing their A-game, but that's my secret: They ALWAYS bring their A-game. The northern lights in that same issue knocked my socks off! And yes, one of my regrets of this series ending is not getting to write Rachel anymore (it was also a very pleasant surprise how fun she is), but there mayyyyyyy be one more appearance and trick up her sleeve...

DEREK: Thanks so much, Craig. I could tell in Ryan's script that sequence was really special, and it was fun to use some different techniques to try to make it stand on its own. And, of course, Rico took it to the next level with his colors. I was legitimately pleased to be working on the only WAR OF THE REALMS tie-in with an extended poetry interlude (followed immediately by a giant named Daisy slapping our heroes across the country).

Dear Ryan, Erica, Rico, Derek, and Wil,

The UNBEATABLE SQUIRREL GIRL is coming to an end. Endings can be sad, but it gives the Holdren family a chance to look back. Back in 2014, with the help of streaming services and DVDs, our then-4-year-old daughter, Iris, had already watched age-appropriate super hero cartoons and loved them. But I could not find a comic that I felt was appropriate and that would catch her attention. When SQUIRREL GIRL was announced, I knew it would be the perfect comic for her.

I sat down with Iris and explained the character and her powers, and then we read and reread the preview pages. Iris was hooked! Then, in a wonderful bit of serendipity, we learned Erica and Rico would be doing a signing of the first issue at our local comic shop, Acme Comics, in Greensboro, NC. When we told Iris we would be meeting them, she thought it would be appropriate to bring gifts and decided to make Erica and Rico beaded necklaces. At the signing, when she met them she said, "I'm your BEST fan!" We hoped they were not annoyed. Iris and I made picking up and reading SQUIRREL GIRL together our monthly routine. When she had questions we would reach out to Erica and Rico and eventually Ryan on Twitter—and often got answered (we like to say that Iris was low-key Twitter famous).

Of course, Iris wanted to dress up as Squirrel Girl for Halloween in 2015, so we made it happen. She won a local kids costume contest. We were also lucky that she did not grow that much between Halloween and the next Free Comic Book Day because she was able to wear the costume one last time to show Erica, who was again a guest of Acme Comics for that event. We also got to see Rico again at several cons in NC.

In the summer of 2017, I got very sick and spe most of the summer in and out of the hospit Iris and her mother (Betsy) kept buying SQUIRRE GIRL, but Iris did not want to read any of the until I was able to read them with her. Eventual I recovered, and we spent a week reading ar getting caught back up with the comic. To top c 2017, you all reached out to us and requeste a drawing from Iris to be included in issue #2 We were so proud and so thankful for the chanc for Iris (who was and still is thrilled by this

During these five years, our 4-year-old turned in a 9-year-old and a current rising fourth grade She learned to read (at least partly by readin SQUIRREL GIRL comics) and reads SQUIRRE GIRL on her own now. Most times she reads th current comic in the car on the way home fro Acme Comics. Iris is well-known at her loc comic shop and the pull box we have there hers. She's had more wonderful experiences du to SQUIRREL GIRL and your creative team tha we could have ever imagined. We will miss yo all greatly, but endings are good because the open up new beginnings. We have included som pictures of Iris' adventures with and as Squirr Girl over the years. Thank you, thank you, thar you. And a special message from Iris herself: do not know what I would have done if I didn have this comic. It's sooo good, and thank yo

Bes
Quinten, Iris, and Betsy Holdre

'AN: I'm so glad you've written in, because it)uldn't have felt right to not have Iris in the ok one more time! It's been such a privilege see her grow with the comic, and to be vited into your house and family—in comic ok form—so often and for so long. She's en reading SQUIRREL GIRL for more than half r life so far: That's incredible! Thank you, Iris. nd your parents have the right idea: to new ginnings. I can't wait to see what you do next.**

EREK: This was really great to read. So mbling to be a small part of something at has such an impact on your lives. I will ep my eyes out for that award-winning quirrel Girl costume at my next comic con!

hat?! No! I just read that issue #50 is the final stallment for this run of THE UNBEATABLE UIRREL GIRL. I know that all good things entually come to an end, but I was more epared for this series to maybe finalize at #400 so. I'm thankful that we got around 60 chapters, cluding the first series and original graphic vel, but I can't help feeling a bit bummed out.

utside of the pure fun of this comic book for readers, it will always hold a special place ithin our family. My 8-year-old twin daughters ve had a blast interacting with y'all over the ars, and it is awesome that they will have e books to look back on when they are much der. As a father, thanks for allowing me to are that with my girls. It is already something at they think is amazing, and I know those ublished experiences will become more golden them as time continues to turn into memories.

s been a killer ride! Everyone involved should e proud of your part in making it all happen. I'm ot stoked that I'm down to my last few sentences at I'll be sending to my favorite Marvel title, ut I'm really happy that I made the decision check it out years ago. You knocked it out of e ballpark. Like if the ballpark was an earlobe n Ego the Living Planet, the ball was a boot om the closet of Thanos, and you all were the eyonder with a bat made out of a bunch of mad Volverines from alternate realities. Great work.

Darrick Patrick
Dayton, Ohio

S. I'm including a photograph of Logann and ola wearing the most recent shirts that have een added to their Squirrel Girl wardrobe. They re going to miss showing you all of their new oreen gear when they get it. Take care, and l our love!

RYAN: And Darrick, it's great to hear from you nd your twins too—they've been SQUIRREL IRL readers from the beginning too! It's so errific. I'm going to miss these letters; thank ou so much for them. Logann and Nola—you ook so powerful and confident in that shot. I'm oing to miss seeing you grow with this comic, ut I know you're going to do amazing things. am excited to find out what they will be! <3

DEREK: Thanks, Darrick. I keep thinking about that analogy you use at the end of this letter and I'm going to have to figure out how to draw it.

USG Crew,

I've been reading comics for 25 years, but never have I encountered anything as hyper-clever and precious as these past 54 issues of UNBEATABLE SQUIRREL GIRL. When I heard it was ending, I had to write my first-ever letter to a comic. I checked the series out because I loved your dry wit through *Dinosaur Comics* and had heard SG was a unique new title; I have never regretted that decision. Ryan, you never fail to make me grin with your barrage of intellectual nuggets, social justice, and Squirrel facts. Your re-imagining of Doreen and development of her supporting cast were on point. You've ALL done Stan's vision for Marvel proud. Cheers (or maybe nuts) to you! (I think it's time we reclaim that phrase as a positive.)

Drew, 32
Wisconsin

RYAN: Drew I'd say your first-ever letter to a comic was a success! It's so gratifying to know you've been reading my stuff since *Dinosaur Comics*—that means I have, POTENTIALLY, been read by you for upwards of a decade! There's no greater compliment you can give a writer. Nuts to you as well, my friend!!

DEREK: Thanks, Drew! Nuts to one and all!

Dearest SQUIRREL GIRL team:

About *cough cough* years ago (way back in issue #5!), I wrote to you expressing our love for this book, and I just wanted to drop another line to express it again as the series comes to a close. My daughter Zoe, now almost 9 years old, has grown up on this series. She's gone to cons dressed as SG, been drawn as an SG Muppet by Guy Gilchrist, drawn her own comics and written her own stories, and developed a pretty sharp sense of right and wrong that I think Doreen has strongly influenced.

The best part may be that, the temporal mechanics of child memory being what they are, she's completely forgotten the early half of the series, so we get to read it all again fresh!

So thanks again for all the great stories, all the great art, all the great memories, and all the great butts.

Alexander and Zoe Burns

PS: Not to make you guys feel bad but Zoe has her own message as well.

RYAN: ZOE!! Your picture is so great! And I love how you used three different text styles for "love." Do I foresee, perhaps, a career or even hobby in lettering comics?? You've got the instinct for it! The good news is, we'll keep making SQUIRREL GIRL for two more issues, and we'll try to make them something you don't forget. And Alexander, the science behind childhood amnesia is so fascinating! Basically, we all forget the first few years of our lives, and we don't really know why. We know that it seems to affect other animals too, but we can't say much beyond that. This basically puts us at about the same place we are with sleep, where we know it happens, we know it's not just us, but we haven't actually nailed down what purpose it serves beyond "stopping us from feeling sleepy." There's theories, but no hard answers! It's so fascinating. And it's also not super squirrel related, so I should probably stop gushing about it here in this letter column, but I am stoked Zoe gets to enjoy the book twice!

DEREK: Ryan, I didn't know any of this (I guess I suspected?), but thanks for educating me even here in the letters section of our comic book. ZOE! That is an amazing drawing, and it sounds like I'll be reading one of your comics someday, and I'm looking forward to it!

Attention, Squirrel Scouts! Make sure to check out our production blog, **unbeatablesquirrelgirl.tumblr.com**, where we post behind-the-scenes stuff on how the book gets made, along with all sorts of cool things *you* make: fanart, cosplay, whatever!

49
EH!
2019

Doreen Green doesn't just study computer science - she also studies **justice,** thanks to her being born with all the powers of a squirrel **and** all the powers of a girl! With the help of her best friends (human and squirrel), she fights crime and saves Earth on the regular. Her pals call her Doreen - which means you can too! - but if you ever see her in costume, keep her secret identity safe and call her...**The Unbeatable Squirrel Girl!**

Squirrel Girl *in a nutshell*

Squirrel Girl @unbeatablesg
GOOD NEWS: I don't have to hide who I am anymore!

Squirrel Girl @unbeatablesg
BAD NEWS: that's because Melissa leaked my secret identity and now villains are coming to attack me lol

Squirrel Girl @unbeatablesg
GOOD NEWS: I got Swarm to stop attacking me!

Squirrel Girl @unbeatablesg
BAD NEWS: now Melissa is attacking me lol

Squirrel Girl @unbeatablesg
GOOD NEWS: Mew survived my apartment blowing up thanks to help from all the squirrels, including Tippy and Archie the Little Squirrel With Fleas!

Squirrel Girl @unbeatablesg
BAD NEWS: my apartment got blown up lol

Squirrel Girl @unbeatablesg
GOOD NEWS: Melissa is alone and unarmed so it should be easy to stop her!!

Squirrel Girl @unbeatablesg
BAD NEWS: uh wait no she's not actually alone and tons of bad guys just teleported in including Doctor Doom lol

Squirrel Girl @unbeatablesg
GOOD NEWS: @starkmantony is here to help me fight these villains!

Squirrel Girl @unbeatablesg
BAD NEWS: Melissa put her own backdoor into Tony's suit source months ago and now she controls ALL his suits, which is really really REALLY bad, and which, i hasten to add: lol

Nancy W. @sewwiththeflo
@unbeatablsg Big into the ironic lols lately huh?

Squirrel Girl @unbeatablesg
@sewwiththeflo some days all you have are the ironic lols!! some days all you can do is summarize bad events and then add "lol" after them

Nancy W. @sewwiththeflo
@unbeatablsg Things look dire lol

Squirrel Girl @unbeatablesg
@sewwiththeflo not sure how we're going to pull this one off lol

Nancy W. @sewwiththeflo
@unbeatablsg Brain Drain's head has been added to a giant scorpion tank that's gonna attack us lol

Squirrel Girl @unbeatablesg
@sewwiththeflo There's so many villains that even if doctor doom wasn't there we'd be pooched but doctor doom IS there, so if i may be so bold: lol

Nancy W. @sewwiththeflo
@unbeatablsg We should probably stop tweeting and get back to this fight lol

Squirrel Girl @unbeatablesg
@sewwiththeflo agreed lol

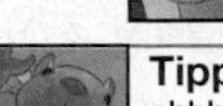
Tippy-Toe @yoitstippytoe
chhht! CHHT CCCT CHHRRRRT!

Tippy-Toe @yoitstippytoe
chrRRRt!

Tippy-Toe @yoitstippytoe
Chrrrt chhhr! ckkk! CHRRT!!

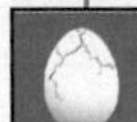
Egg @imduderadtude
@yoitstippytoe now THIS is the online content i crave

search! 

- #fullissuefightscene
- #tropicalyellows
- #eeniemeanieminey
- #beunbeatable
- #accomplishtwothings

In case you were wondering, the reference he makes on this page *does* establish in canon that Taskmaster's favorite Broadway musical is 1946's Irving Berlin-penned *Annie Get Your Gun.* Taskmaster isn't just a guy with a skull for a face who can duplicate skills just from seeing them once--he *also* loves musical theatre.

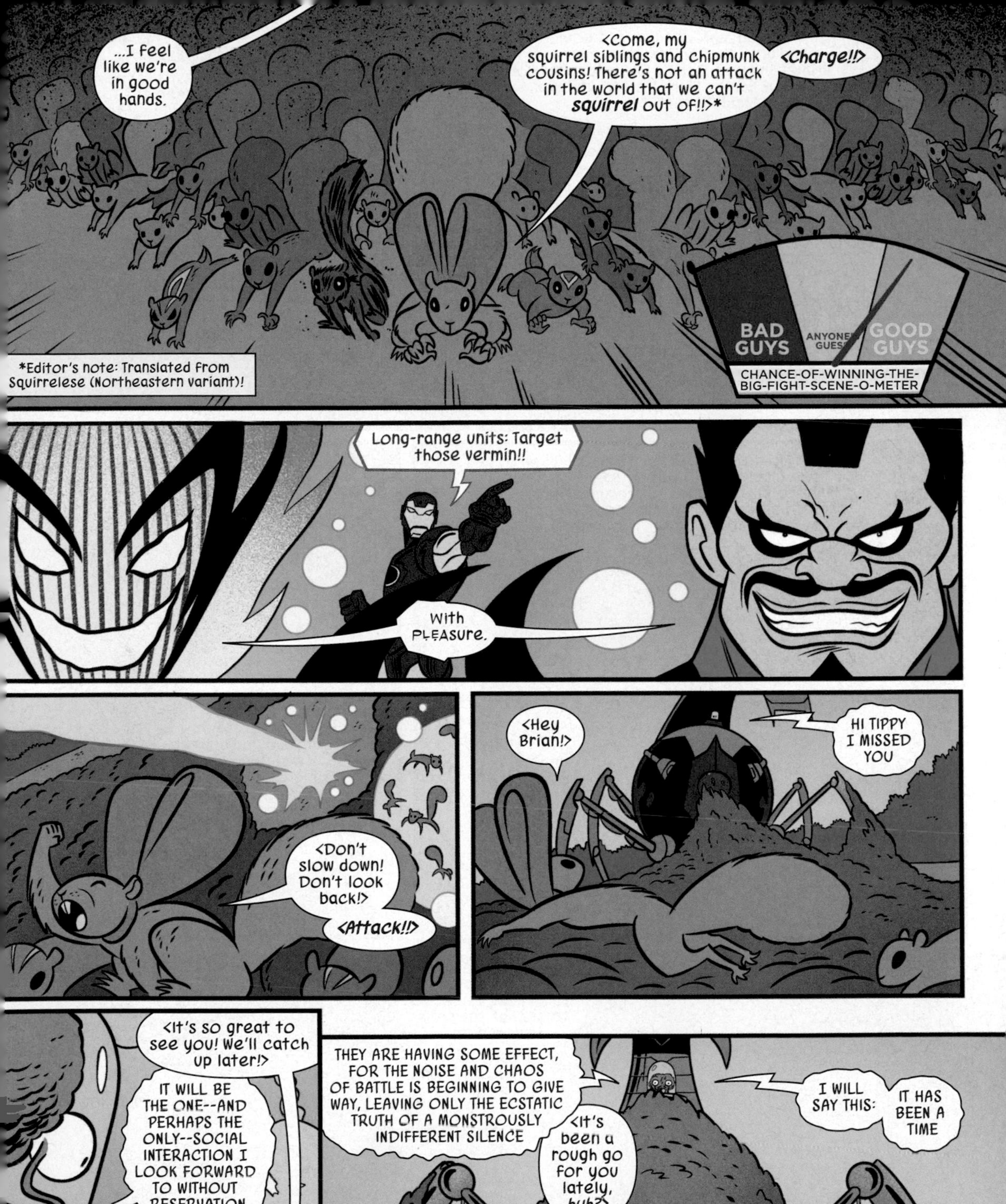
...I feel like we're in good hands.
<Come, my squirrel siblings and chipmunk cousins! There's not an attack in the world that we can't **squirrel** out of!!>*
<Charge!!>
BAD GUYS
GOOD GUYS
CHANCE-OF-WINNING-THE-BIG-FIGHT-SCENE-O-METER
*Editor's note: Translated from Squirrelese (Northeastern variant)!
Long-range units: Target those vermin!!
With PLEASURE.
<Don't slow down! Don't look back!>
<Attack!!>
<Hey Brian!>
HI TIPPY I MISSED YOU

<It's so great to see you! We'll catch up later!>
IT WILL BE THE ONE--AND PERHAPS THE ONLY--SOCIAL INTERACTION I LOOK FORWARD TO WITHOUT RESERVATION
<Love it. The squirrels are going to try to block your body's sensors, okay?>
THEY ARE HAVING SOME EFFECT, FOR THE NOISE AND CHAOS OF BATTLE IS BEGINNING TO GIVE WAY, LEAVING ONLY THE ECSTATIC TRUTH OF A MONSTROUSLY INDIFFERENT SILENCE
<It's been a rough go for you lately, *huh?*>
I WILL SAY THIS:
IT HAS BEEN A TIME

Did you know that the first ever squirrel census in Central Park was recently run (by humans)? The result: An estimated 2,373 eastern gray squirrels live in Central Park. And Doctor Doom and Melissa Morbeck have just ***cheesed them all off.***

Confound these wretched rodents! For every one I fling away at a distance with these gauntlet blasts, a dozen more ***vex*** me!
Doom will only comment thusly: There's something oddly familiar about all this!

Meanwhile Chipmunk Hunk's inner voice is telling him to be cool while his other internal voice is screaming
We just punched Doctor Doom, ahhh, this is amazing, did anyone see this, we even had a line ready to go for it this is amazing

KRAKK
Foolish animals! You may be able to attack *en masse*, but you will all fall alone when **Baron Mordo** calls down his...
Muddling mind-mists...
...of Mkah'thuth!!
ZZZZZT
BAD GUYS
ANYONE'S GUESS
GOOD GUYS
CHANCE-OF-WINNING-THE-BIG-FIGHT-SCENE-O-METER
BAD GUYS
ANYONE'S GUESS
GOOD GUYS
CHANCE-OF-WINNING-THE-BIG-FIGHT-SCENE-O-METER
<Eugh. So--dizzy!>
<Can't... balance...!>
<Bleh.>
Hah! That spell may only work on *smaller* minds, but it's more than enough against these--these little *trash mammals!*
Oh my god. You did not just say that.
You did **not** just **say** that!
I'll be accepting your apology now, Baron Mordo!!
<World... spinning!... Can't...see... clearly...>
<Or...speak... without...dramatic... pauses...>
<Must...bite... correct...final...wire! Must... save...Brian...!>
<Eenie... meanie...miney...!>
...moe, catch a tiger by the toe, if he hollers let him go, eenie meanie miney...

Just want to point out that with this book ending soon, Brain Drain will be more available to make appearances in other books.
Attention other Marvel writers: Do not let this opportunity slip through your fallible, all-too-human fingers.

Sometimes you seize the day, and sometimes the day seizes back and hits you with two of your best friends.

Time to lay down the Fin Fang *boom.*
AHHHHH!
SMAK
AHHHHHH!
AHHHH--
--wait. Wait!

The cavalry's here!
I think that's quite enough of that, *Iron Ring.*
SMAK

It's so far up my alley that if you type in "Mary Mahajan" into Google it already autocompletes to "Mary Mahajan doomsday scorpion tank." And if it doesn't...it's about to.

Ah well, just an odd noise in a room filled with weapons. It's probably ***Fine.*** *It's probably fine! Let the guards guard and the worriers worry, that's what I, a guard, always say!*

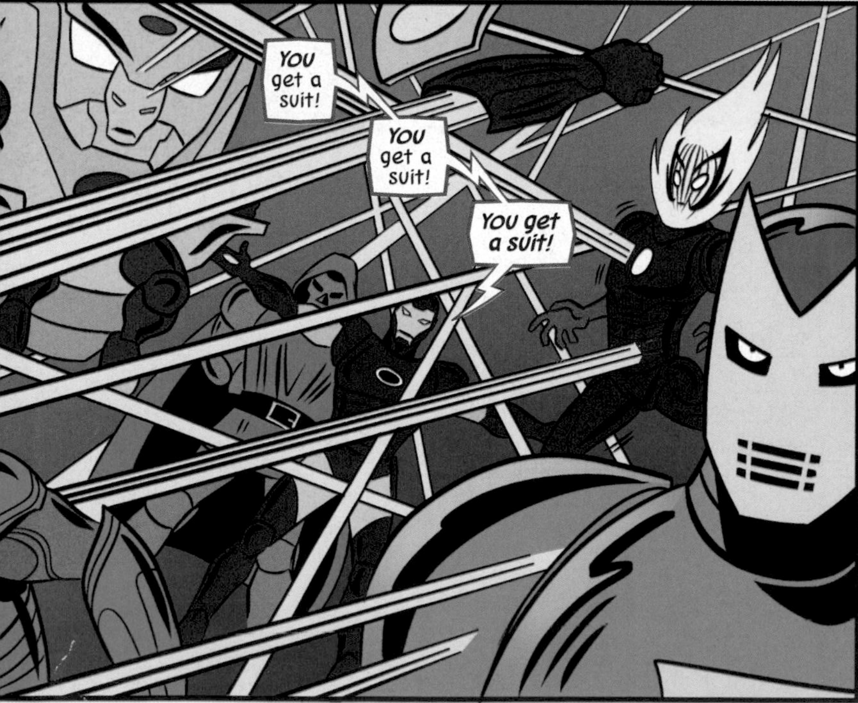

You already have your birthday suit, Tony.

Oh, this will work out quite nicely. Let's see you go for the head now, Avengers!!
I could get used to this.
BAD GUYS
ANYONE'S GUESS
GOOD GUYS
CHANCE-OF-WINNING-THE-BIG-FIGHT-SCENE-O-METER

Melissa! Doom!
Stop this!!

SNATCH!
Hrrk!

Before you say it, Doom: Yes, I could've led with the armor. But I think you'll agree that this way--where you can actually see the hope fade from her eyes--is better.
You may prove yourself yet, Ms. Morbeck.
I just might.

This is where your story ends, Squirrel Girl.
Maybe, but...that's not hope... fading from my eyes...

Oh? What is it then?
It's... nothing. Just...
...just...

...just a distraction.
Behind you, Vic.

Surpriiise.

A few weeks from now Melissa is going to be annoyed when the great "Funny: I never heard of *squirrels* playing possum before" line finally comes to her.

Captain Marvel's "binary powers" refer to when she gains the powers of a white hole (a speculative space-time structure that spews out light and matter, the opposite of a black hole) and do *not*, in fact, refer to when she gains the powers of a really good computer. Sometimes comics aren't perfect! I don't know what to tell you!

SMAK
SMAK
SMAK
SMAK
SMAK
SMAK
KA-SMAK
Friends... losing fight... gotta...get up...
Gotta...be unbeatable...
Gotta--
...gotta...
I must say: If you truly needed my help *this* badly...
...who...?

...then Belka, why did you not simply *say* so?
Kraven!!
The Avengers aren't the only ones with an ear to the ground, platonic m'lady.
It's *so good* to see you, bud.
Always a pleasure, Doreen.
All right! Listen *up*, everyone!!
We're all here because we want to help Squirrel Girl, who is apparently *not* named "Scarlett," but we can talk about that later!
You know what I heard? I heard all the bad guys here said we were *big suckers* who couldn't beat them. *Are you gonna let that stand??*
Your mission is to hunt Doreen's enemies, who are now *your* enemies too. You each have your own unique skills, and I will not presume to tell you how to use them.
But I will give you this advice. In this coming battle, you must accomplish only *two things,* my friends:

You must eat nuts...
...and you must kick butts!!
BAD GUYS
ANYONE'S GUESS
GOOD GUYS
CHANCE-OF-WINNING-THE-BIG-FIGHT-SCENE-O-METER

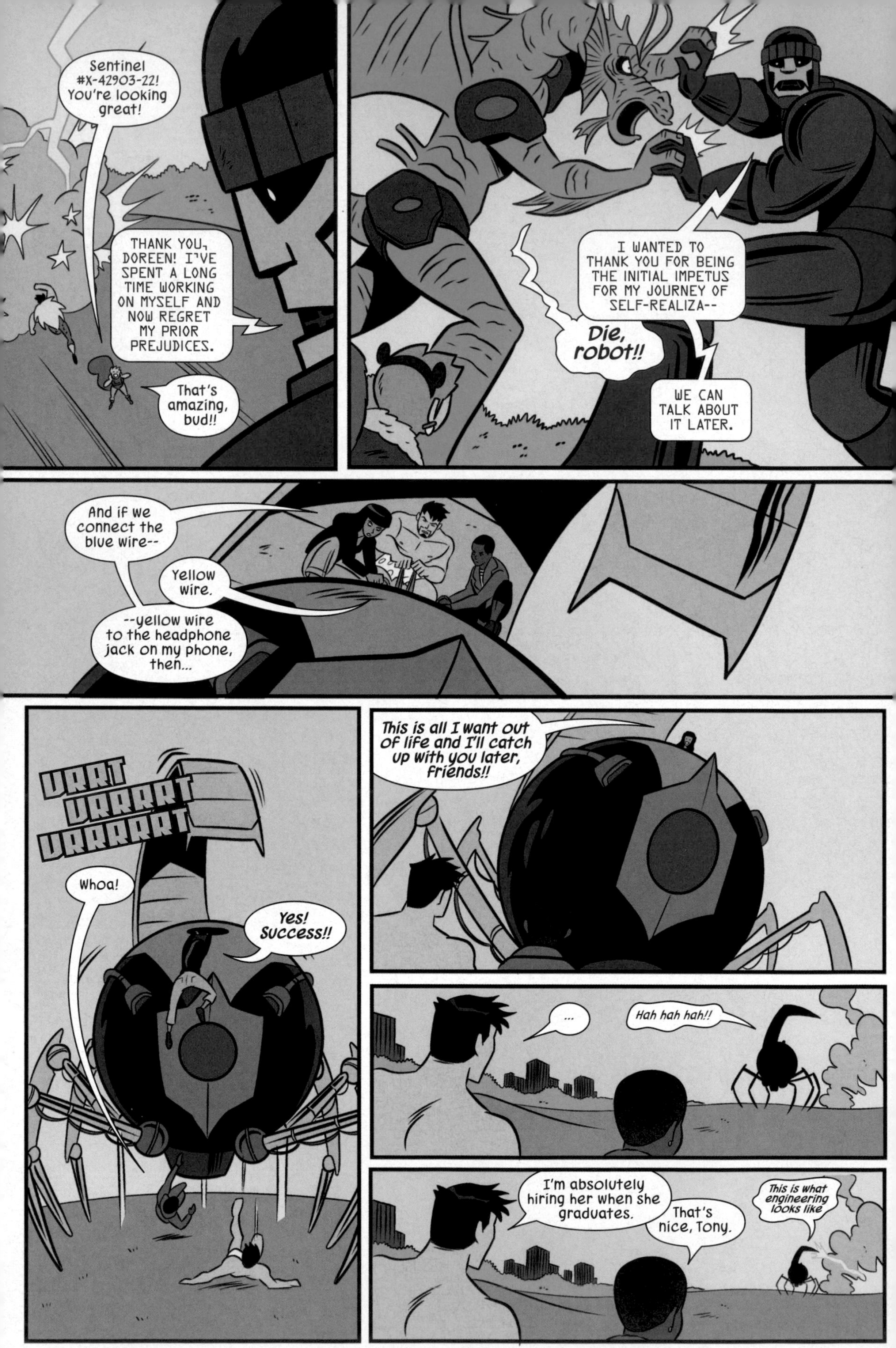

In Mary's defense, this *is* literally what engineering looks like.

Doom being so petty as to always and without exception put the "Captain" part of Captain Marvel's name in quotes may not be the sole reason he's a super villain, but honestly? It doesn't hurt.

Chhhhhtttt!
Chhhhtttt!
Chhhhtttt!
Chhhhtttt!
Chhhhtttt!
What's got the squirrels so upset?
Oh my God.
NO.
Chhhhtttt!
Avengers! There's a bomb somewhere in this field!
Friends, hunt that bomb! Destroy it!
Hah! They're lying. There's no bomb. If it were true, my perfect and calculating brain would've predicted Doom betraying us and--
...oh wait, no, never mind, this absolutely scans and there's literally a 0% chance he's not betraying us as we speak.
DOOM!!
Find the bomb, idiots!
I'm looking, idiot!!
You don't want to spend your last moments futilely searching for my bomb, Ms. Morbeck?
It doesn't matter.
Correct.

"The End"...of THIS issue, we mean! Please don't stop reading here while saying, "oh well, everyone is clearly dead, I guess that's clearly the end of both this book and a large percentage of the shared Marvel Universe!" It's just an amazing cliffhanger and there're still at least 20 more pages of comics to come!! We PROMISE.

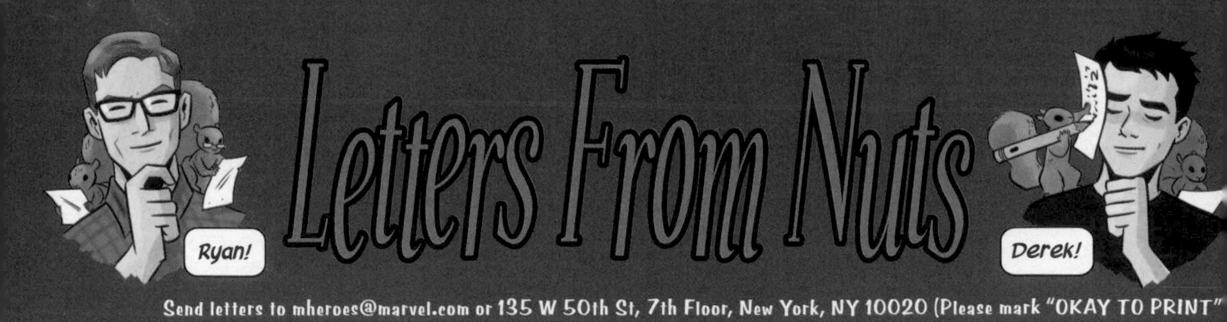

Felicitations to the Squirrel Team—we are Proofreading!

How many hours of our lives have been spent proofreading this book with a magnifying glass? NOT ENOUGH, WE SAY. We may never have perfect eyesight again, but we'll always have the memories (and the Deadpool cards—so many Deadpool cards).

Love,
Jacque, Elissa, Kristin, and Dan
Marvel Proofreading

RYAN: TEAM PROOFREADING!! How ARE you? And I'm sorry for all the little mistakes I've inadvertently added over the years. Or perhaps... intentionally added so that your jobs would not be boring where you just rubber-stamp "YEP, LOOKS GREAT!" on everything?? So, if you think about it, we're BOTH the heroes. But, yes, thank you so much! I have tried so many times to catch all the errors in a script before I submit it, and something always gets through, which makes it thanks to you that Squirrel Girl says, "eat nuts, kick butts!" and not "eta acorns, kick bottoms [tk: make this rhyme before submittikng!!]."

DEREK: Ah! You are all amazing, thank you so much!

Dear Squirrel Girl (and Ryan and Derek and Rico and Erica and everyone else on this wonderful comic's creative team, currently and formerly),

I tried writing a long letter describing how much I've loved the character of Squirrel Girl in this series and the series itself, but I realized I'll never be able to do it all justice. I started reading the series with (the first) #1 because even though I had never bought a comic book before, I'm a longtime fan of Ryan from his *Dinosaur Comics* days, and I never looked back. It's just such a perfect combination of action, humor, intelligence, and heart that I've never seen before. I'm sorry to see the series end but so happy I was able to have it, and you know I'll be following Squirrel Girl's next adventures!

So long and thanks for all the nuts,

Justin, A.K.A. your Friendly Neighborhood Platypus Man

RYAN: Platypus Man, thank you! I'm thrilled that we got to be your first comic book and even more thrilled that we won't be your last. Whether webcomics or print comics, it's all comics, and I love this medium so much, and I'm so flattered you've come along with me from *Dinosaur Comics* to Marvel Comics!

DEREK: Thanks for the kind words, Justin, A.K.A. Platypus Man! That's so awesome this was your first comic!

Dear Ryan, Erica, Rico, Derek, Wil, and the many underrated others I tragically forgot to mention, Thank you all. I started reading with Volume 1 #2 back when I was 15. Now a sophomore in college, it's wild to think how many important parts of my life Doreen has been there for. I've appreciated interacting with y'all on Twitter, and my friends have appreciated my constant rants of praise, eventually turning into theirs following my recommendation of the book! I can honestly say that it was perhaps Doreen more than almost anyone else who set me up to be the person I am today. The compassion, friendship, and fun captured in every issue truly reached me and taught me the same way Doreen taught her villains and friends alike. Congrats on running so long! Unfortunately, I haven't been able to keep up recently for monetary reasons, but buying each issue was always my favorite part of every month.

I'd like to share a story with y'all I've been waiting to for two and a half years. I went to a comic book store for my 17th birthday and of course the latest UNBEATABLE SQUIRREL GIRL was the main priority. That issue was #16, the 25th anniversary issue. As you might imagine, Doreen celebrating her birthday at same time as me was pretty hype. That time was also the hardest period I went through in high school. That issue became a point of stability in an anxious and inconsistent day-to-day that I went back to time and time again. Monkey Joe telling Doreen she's too young to decide there are things she can't do, her finding her confidence and developing friendship, and her final toast thanking her friends with true gratitude for being there for her because she didn't always think she'd have people like that were moments that drew resonant tears from me many lonely times. They gave me hope.

I'm really going to miss USG, and I know each of you will too. But the impact and legacy Doreen and friends had on me is something I think I'll always carry. You've done good work. Thank you. Wish the gang good luck for me!

Sincerely,
West

RYAN: Aw heck, West, thank you. When you write something, you never know what's going to happen to it—if people will read it, if people will care, if it'll find an audience now or later or maybe never—but the best-case scenario, the absolute best-case scenario for any piece of writing, is that someone finds it and reads it and it changes their life for the better. I'm so glad our take on Doreen could be that for you. High school can be hard—especially now, I don't think the older generation always realizes how much things have changed—and if our comics helped even a little, then I am HERE FOR IT, and I really appreciate your letter. That line MJ had about not deciding there are things you can't do when you're young: It's one of my favorites, and it kinda surprised me. I knew I wanted him to say something inspiring in that scene but had no idea what it was until it was there on the screen. I love it when that happens. All the best—and remember that the books are available for free at your local library! (Or at least, once they're collected into trades they will be—soon, soon!)

DEREK: Thanks so much, West. One thing I do like about a run on a comic series being finished is I can read it at my own pace and not have to worry about falling behind. I read issue #16 again recently for some research on Squirrel Girl's parents, and I agree that it's one of the best.

Hello,

Three years ago, I was just getting into reading comics regularly and heard of a title called THE UNBEATABLE SQUIRREL GIRL that intrigued me because I had a friend who had adopted two baby squirrels her children found hurt. It immediately made me think of her, so I checked it out and fell in love with the stories and characters and the extra text on the bottom of the pages. Since then it has become, consistently, one of my all-time favorite books. I read the trades or issues as I get them, and I will dearly miss this run and having new issues to read. However, I have plenty of great stories now to reread and cherish. Issue #31 is the most beautiful story of friendship I have ever read and makes me cry just skimming through it again, and the silent issue makes my librarian heart happy looking through it once more.

Thank you for these stories. I will keep sharing them with my patrons at the library and every kid in my life. And I look forward to seeing Doreen Green again wherever else she crops up in the Marvel Universe.

Mariah Busher
Dayton, OH

RYAN: Mariah, I did not intentionally mention libraries in the last letter, but yours could not be better timed! I'm glad you liked the silent librarian issue—it was a lot of fun (and a big challenge!), and while we couldn't incorporate EVERYTHING librarians do these days (you have such an important job for society, that's what I think; I love librarians, and I will never take this back), it was fun to at least touch on the book aspects! Thank you for sharing Doreen with the people in your world.

DEREK: That's awesome to hear, Mariah—thank you so much!

Hello, Team SG (do you call yourselves Team SG?)! My name is Anton, and this year was confusingly fast in terms of finding the best comic book ever and then a couple months later finding out that this comic book is going to end this very year.

Actually, I knew about USG when it just started. Back then, I saw a few panels and thought, Ugh, this is stupid! Why are they doing it? But thank you so, so much for doing it. It's just ridiculous how one comic book about a girl who is also part squirrel can actually change the real world for the better. Well, I definitely have changed. I try not to hate anyone and anything anymore because that's the most revolutionary thing I can do, actually. And that's just me, but how many more people have changed for the better too? Okay, now I'm crying, so this letter will be short, I guess.

I just want to thank everyone who has ever worked on this comic for everything. You all gave me more emotions and feels and excitement than any other thing in the world. Oh, special thanks for Squirrel Girl's Twitter; I hope you won't abandon it after the last issue! Her Twitter is actually a reason why I started to read USG! Another special thanks for Kraven! His arc is so great! May I say something to him in Russian?

Привет, Сергей! Как же приятно видеть, что ты стараешься стать лучше и порядочнее. Глядя на тебя, я тоже стараюсь. Вот бы ты ещё перестал охотиться на Человека-Паука, он один из моих любимых героев! Уверен, ты видел советский мультфильм, где охотничий пёс стал фотографом, может тебе тоже попробовать?

Okay, thanks again guys, and I hope you will return for some special issue each year or something.

Bye!

Anton Danilov, from Russia with love
(yes, I actually said it, so what!)

RYAN: Anton, thank you—this was great. And your message to Kraven—easy for ME to read since I can copy and paste it into a translator—was sweet too

I admit that I do help out Squirrel Girl with her tweets. While I expect she'll be around (but maybe a little less active), there's always my personal @ryanqnorth account too! Thank you for sharing this comic with us.

DEREK: Anton, thanks so much. That's so awesome that this book has helped shape the way you interact with the world. It's done a similar thing for me as well. Not to eavesdrop on a private conversation, but I also translated your message to Kraven, and I feel like he'd appreciate the encouragement!

USG Team,

I've been reading USG since the beginning, and my niece just turned 5 this year, so I knew the perfect gift for her birthday: a subscription to THE UNBEATABLE SQUIRREL GIRL! My grandma got me a subscription to UNCANNY X-MEN when I was 9, and I can't express just how happy I am to pass along my love of comics to the next generation. My niece loves story time when I come to visit, especially when I try to do the voices of every character as I read to her. USG has always been my favorite to read because it's funny, wholesome, and just darn adorable. I love that Doreen solves problems with friendship, knowledge, and cunning as opposed to jumping right into fisticuffs with some dastardly villain.

Ryan, in an age where long runs on titles are extremely rare (move over, Jason Aaron!), it's amazing that you've had such a great run over a long period of time. Thank you for crafting such a fantastic world and supporting cast. Your Kraven will always be my Kraven. I hope you bring the footnotes with you to the next book you write.

Derek, you had huge shoes to fill when you started on this book, and you've surpassed my high expectations. I can't wait to see what you do next.

Erica, there's not much to say that hasn't already been said. Some creators get an instant buy from me when their name is on the cover, like Morrison, Zdarsky, Hickman, and now Henderson. Rico, your colors are gorgeous. Everything pops off the page, and it looks great in print and on my tablet.

Wil and Sarah, thank you for keeping this series going for as long as it has and especially for keeping the letters page alive. I'm looking forward to gifting TPBs of this series to friends and family for many years to come.

Thank you all for such a wonderful series. It's always at the top of my stack, and I've loved every single issue. I'm going to miss new stories with this cast in this corner of the Marvel Universe, but I'm so grateful for the time we all had together.

Chris McKimmons

RYAN: Chris—thank you! I am SO INTERESTED in knowing what your voices for our characters sound like. Doreen? Nancy? BRAIN DRAIN? Well, that last one is easy, since in my head he always sounds like Werner Herzog, and I read all his lines out loud doing my best Herzog impression to make sure they scan. And thank you for the kind words about Kraven—he quickly became one of my favorite characters too, and I'm glad we got to bring him back for this last arc. (Surprise! And, uh, spoiler alert if you're for some reason reading the letters page before the issue itself!) If I can praise Derek a bit here too: The script for this issue was insane, with 30+ characters all in the same scene, and man, you drew the heck out of it. It's so impressive!!

DEREK: Thank you so much, Chris (AND RYAN!). Following Erica on this book was extremely intimidating, and I have everyone you listed here to thank for helping me get where I needed to be. Ryan's also constantly pushing me to draw things I never would have thought myself capable of, which is one of my favorite things about working with him. (BTW, drawing 30 characters isn't as hard as remembering what each of them wears from panel to panel. I don't know how those X-Men artists do it!)

Hey, Squirrel-Ryan and Derek-Nuts,

It's me, Marius, from Denmark again!! Hope it's okay I'm writing another letter. I'm very sad about your stopping. I now give orders to not stop. If you refuse, Gary and Danielle will come and attack Ryan until he begins to write more issues. I really hope that #50 will be a legendary issue, but it's you who make it, so it cannot be bad. But as the genius I am, I have made some more questions:

1. Who is Squirrel Girl's archenemy?

2. Will Egg's identity be revealed?

3. Maybe the Frosted Flakes were Roxxon's work?

4. How many powers does Ratatoskr have?

5. Who is the strongest Frost Giant?

From your Squirrel Friend,
Marius

RYAN: Thank you, Marius! To answer your questions:

1) I think it's Melissa Morbeck, maybe tied for first with Doom!

2) It is a random egg whose identity will remain shrouded in mystery!

3) Ooh, I like this theory.

4) Ratatoskr has mind control and shape-shifting powers, along with some other powers that support it. And maybe a few tricks up her sleeve?

5) I don't know who the strongest Frost Giant is, but if nobody else has claimed it, let's say Danielle! I declare this CANON.

DEREK: Ratatoskr also has the power of being my favorite character to draw who is not BRAIN DRAIN.

Hello, Squirrel Girl people.

With the upcoming end of THE UNBEATABLE SQUIRREL GIRL, I'd been thinking about writing you folks another letter—and then I saw online that the final story arc begins with Brain Drain missing...Well, as I'll explain, THAT was too great a bit of cosmic irony for me to ignore, hence this letter.

I create custom LEGO figures, and long ago, you were kind enough to publish pictures of my versions of Squirrel Girl, Nancy, Tippy-Toe, and Mew. This spring, I had operations on both eyes to remove cataracts, and I can't do such custom work these days. The last figures I finished beforehand were a trio of Brain Drain figures: one for me, one for Ryan, and one for Erica. Here's a picture of mine:

The dome is made from a cut-down plastic test tube, while the brain and eyes are scratch-built from epoxy putty and wire and then painted. (That work was done with only one useful eye, since I'd already had my first operation at that point.) I'm happy with the results, and Ryan and Erica seemed pleased too at TCAF 2019.

So, what's the great cosmic irony? Last month, the dome/brain of my Brain Drain went missing, just as I was installing a display of my work at the Ottawa Public Library. Arrrrgh! So I'm hoping that there's going to be a whole bunch of happy reunions involving Brain Drain at some point in my future. Sigh.

Thanks to all of the hardworking and creative people who have made USG such a delight. It's been an honor to have my own contributions be a part of the letters page.

Regards,
Norbert Black
Ottawa, Ontario, Canada

RYAN: Norbert, it was a pleasure to meet you at various shows, and I wanted to share this pic of the Brain Drain you gave me defending the city from the threat of Giant 3D-Printed Me looming behind him. Brian here is my #1 favorite LEGO figure of all time, and I'm so flattered you gave him to me. I wish you the speediest of recoveries from your surgeries!!

DEREK: Norbert, this is awesome, and my first instinct is to say, "I want one," but reading how much work you put into these, I will be satisfied asking Ryan to bring it with him whenever he travels in case we run into each other so I can see it in person and marvel at a three-dimensional Brain Drain.

Next: The Final Issue!!!

Attention, Squirrel Scouts! Make sure to check out our production blog, **unbeatablesquirrelgirl.tumblr.com**, where we post behind-the-scenes stuff on how the book gets made, along with all sorts of cool things *you* make: fanart, cosplay, whatever!

50
EH! 2019

Doreen survived the blast.
She is--resilient. But while our allies ran away from the explosion, she and her fellow "heroes" foolishly ran toward it. We remain undamaged and they are weakened. It will now be trivial to finish them off.
Again, and always...Doom triumphs.

Easy, Doreen, easy--
We need to get her to a hospital.
We all are in need of one. My van can hold some, but--
No. We stay. Someone has to stop Melissa and Doom, because if we can't...

PWEEE
...nobody will.
You're out of tricks--and friends. Goodbye, Doreen.

Call yourself "unbeatable" all you want, but you can't change reality:
All the friendship on Earth can't save you now.
KRACKA CHOOM

Get to safety! NOW!
Doreen, you can't--
NO!
KA-CHOOOO

OOOM

Um. Everything's...
...purple?

WELL THEN
I SUPPOSE IT'S A GOOD THING THAT NOT ALL HER FRIENDS LIVE ON EARTH, ISN'T IT
Galactus! Buddy!
OH IT IS ON NOW--and that's not even Galactus speaking! I'M JUST SO EXCITED AT HOW ON IT CURRENTLY IS THAT I CAN ONLY PROPERLY EXPRESS MYSELF IN ALL CAPS!!

Thanks for blocking that shot! It's *so good* to see you, man!

Holy carp.
Da. As you apparently say in America: "Holy carp."

Okay. *Okay.* We can work with this, right? You've got something up your sleeve that can beat him. Doom always triumphs, right?
Correct, Ms. Morbeck. Doom *always* triumphs.
Eventually.

But Doom also recognizes that *discretion* is the better part of *valor.*
No, you can't *leave* me here! It's *Galactus!!*

Goodbye, Ms. Morbeck. You are unlikely to survive the day. But die with this satisfaction: You *were--* ever so briefly--*useful* to Doom.
Victor!!

To be fair, very few people have ever been useful to Doom, so that is technically about as close to giving a compliment as he gets.

FRANKLY THE FACT THAT SOME OF YOU HAVE REMAINED UNDEVOURED FOR SO LONG IS A CONSTANT SUBJECT OF DISCUSSION ON THE DEVOURERS OF WORLDS MESSAGE BOARDS AND DISCORD CHANNELS

OKAY, I'VE DONE AS YOU'VE ASKED: TIME IS OUT, AND CAUSALITY IS FROZEN FOR EVERYONE BUT US
WHAT'S UP, DOREEN

Galactus buddy, I really appreciate your help here, but you can't just eat people!
PRETTY SURE THAT I CAN
No, I mean--like, in the permissive sense! We need to talk about this!!

You and me, Galactus. The moon. Now.
BUT--
NOW.

SO
I BELIEVE THERE WAS SOMETHING YOU WANTED TO DISCUSS
Whoa, you fixed my battle damage!

Thanks Galactus! That's rad!
I ALSO MADE IT SO YOU CAN BREATHE IN SPACE. BUT IS THIS JUST FOR NOW, OR IS IT A PERMANENT POWER BOOST??
I'LL NEVER TELL
BUT I DON'T UNDERSTAND WHY YOU WANTED ME TO STOP, DOREEN. I THOUGHT WE WERE FRIENDS AND YOU NEEDED MY HELP
Oh, I'm more than happy to accept your help--believe me!--but you can't just kill everyone! That's what Doom wanted. And any solution that involves murder isn't a solution, man!
Heck, any solution that involves "doing what Doctor Doom would do" isn't a solution. That's like page one of the super hero manual.

That "don't do what Doctor Doom does" advice comes from an inspirational poster Doreen bought for Mary. It's great because it seems like a really cool poster until you interrogate why someone would need to be reminded not to behave like Doctor Doom *so often* that they have a poster about it on their wall!

TO ANSWER YOUR QUESTION, YES, THE POWER COSMIC CAN MAKE A ROCK SO HEAVY THAT EVEN THE POWER COSMIC CANNOT LIFT IT, AND YES, THE POWER COSMIC DOES THIS CONSTANTLY. THE POWER COSMIC IS *THAT GOOD*

EARTH MORALS ARE WEIRD AND COMPLICATED BUT I SUPPOSE SPACE MORALS MIGHT BE TOO IF YOU WEREN'T RAISED WITH THEM
I guess?
Earth morality is largely based around determining how one ought to live at the individual level, and we--
BUT THEY'RE WHAT YOU WANT, SO I'M WILLING TO PLAY ALONG AND DO AS YOU ASK, DOREEN. WE WILL SOLVE THIS TOGETHER
Well--great! That, uh--that entirely resolves the whole big fight scene we had going on!
INDEED IT DOES
Nobody dies today!
CORRECT
This is nice. Thank you, Galactus.
THIS IS NICE. THIS IS VERY NICE
AND I'M REALLY GOING TO MISS IT
I'M GOING TO MISS YOU TOO, DOREEN GREEN
I--I don't understand. Are you going away for a while? Am I?
What's going on, Galactus?
I know, I know, it's super unfair to drop an incredible concept like "space morals" in our last issue and not explore it further! But you gotta leave some bread crumbs for future creative teams to pick up on, right?

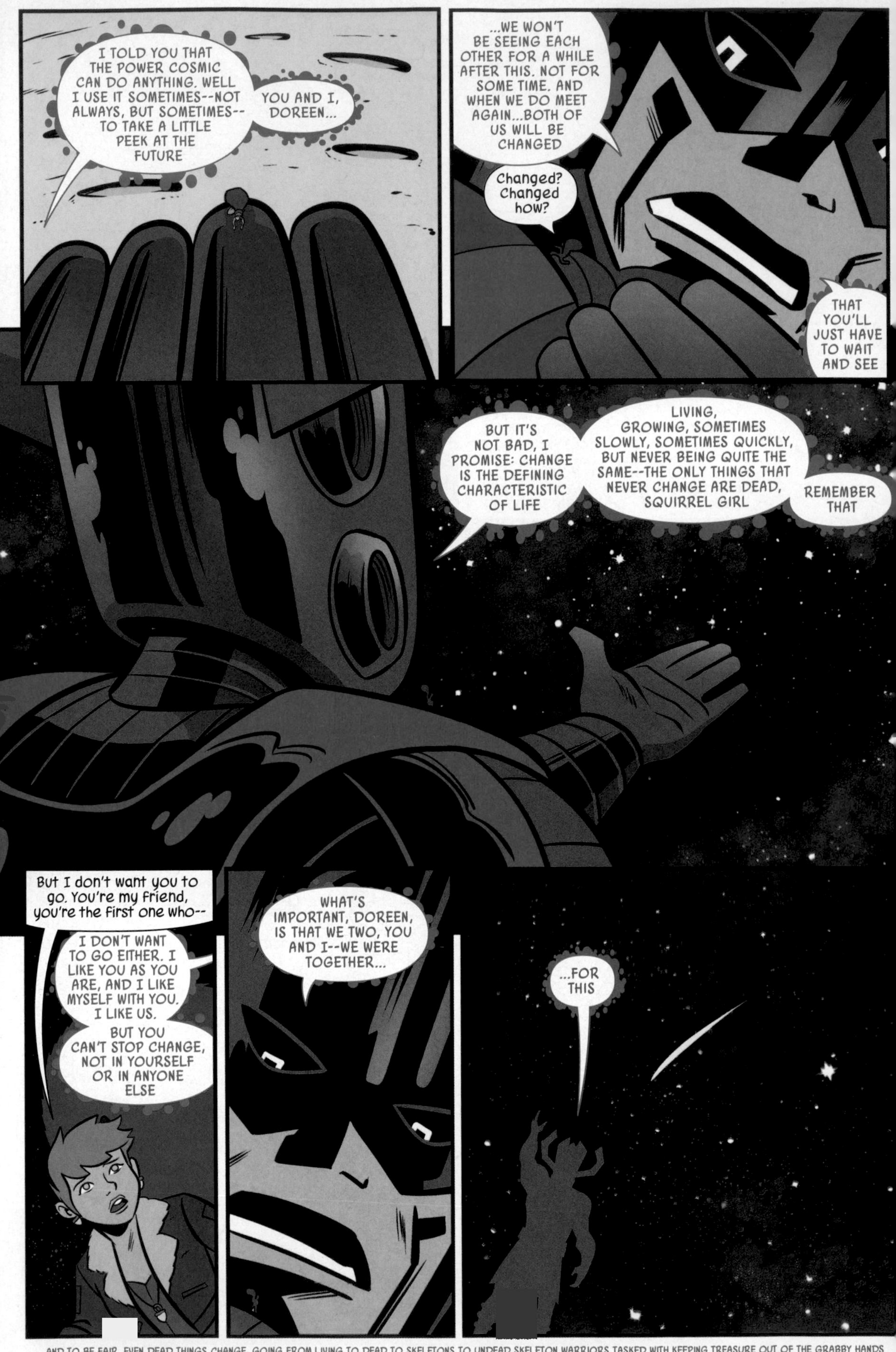

AND TO BE FAIR, EVEN DEAD THINGS CHANGE, GOING FROM LIVING TO DEAD TO SKELETONS TO UNDEAD SKELETON WARRIORS TASKED WITH KEEPING TREASURE OUT OF THE GRABBY HANDS OF ADVENTURERS TO DEFEATED SKELETON WARRIORS PLAYING CARDS WITH EACH OTHER TO PASS THE TIME--IT'S ALL PART OF THE BEAUTIFUL CONTINUUM OF LIFE

"This"?
I WANT TO TELL YOU SOMETHING I HAVEN'T TOLD ANYONE ELSE BEFORE: WHEN YOU WIELD THE POWER COSMIC, YOU DON'T JUST GET TO SEE THE FUTURE
YOU CAN SEE THE PAST AND PRESENT DIFFERENTLY TOO
AND WHEN YOU DO, YOU KNOW THAT THIS MOMENT, AND ALL THOSE THAT CAME BEFORE IT--EVERYTHING IN THIS UNIVERSE, EVERYTHING WE'VE SHARED FROM THE VERY BEGINNING OF OUR STORIES--WILL ALWAYS EXIST, READY TO BE REVISITED BY THOSE WITH THE POWER TO SEE IT
SOME WILL SEEK US OUT OFTEN, TO REMEMBER HOW WE--AND THEY--ONCE WERE
SOME MAY FIND US ONLY BY CHANCE, REACHING OUT FROM SOME DISTANT FUTURE THAT HAS ALL BUT FORGOTTEN OUR LIVES
AND WE WILL BE THERE, WAITING FOR THEM. WE ALREADY ARE, DOREEN. AND WHEN THEY COME, WE WILL DO IT ALL AGAIN, EXACTLY AS IT HAPPENED THE FIRST TIME
WE WERE HERE WHEN IT HAPPENED, AND THAT'S WHAT MAKES THIS MOMENT SPECIAL. BUT THERE WILL ALWAYS BE THOSE WHO WILL COME AFTER US AND WHO WILL WANT TO KNOW WHAT IT WAS LIKE
...what *what* was like?
WHAT IT WAS LIKE...

...WHEN SQUIRREL GIRL AND GALACTUS FIRST MET ON THE MOON

THIS ISN'T FAIR! I BARELY EVEN PARTICIPATED!!

Who makes a cell designed to be immune to *all* our abilities?

Doreen!!

Doom demands a diplomatic envoy!!
Doom left the battlefield early and therefore already pre-emptively denied all culpability, jailkeep!!

Doom would like to clarify that any illegal activities for which he is unjustly being held were actually performed by a rogue robot, clone, or simulacrum! ***Blame them!!***

Captain America hasn't heard about *any* of these prior interactions of Doreen and Galactus, so he is just completely floored. ***As well he should be: They were amazing.***

That Russian saying, literally translated, means, "They say they milk chickens."
I will say this: "They say they milk chickens" is a ***way*** more memorable way to express skepticism than saying "don't believe everything you hear."
And that's not just me milking chickens!!

It's so weird to look at the wreckage of our apartment like this--it feels like we're looking at the wreckage of our lives, you know?
Pshaw.

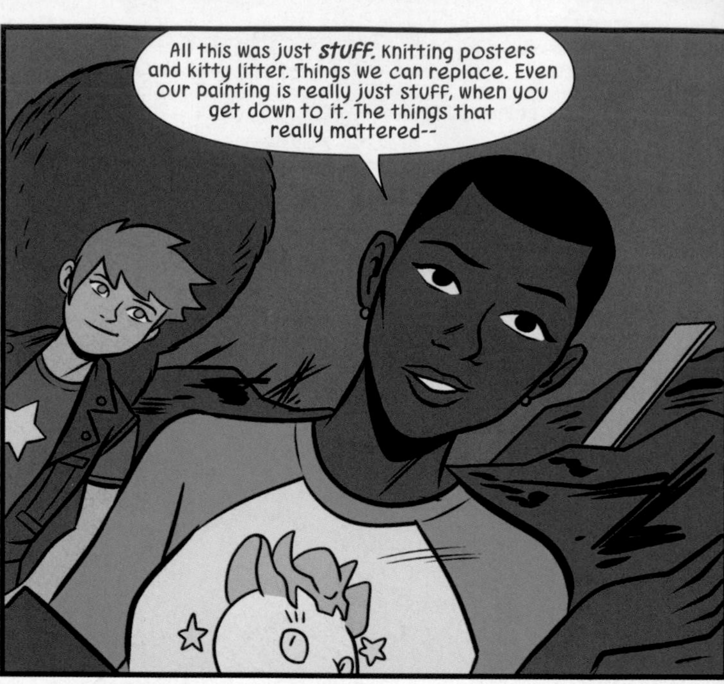

All this was just STUFF. Knitting posters and kitty litter. Things we can replace. Even our painting is really just stuff, when you get down to it. The things that really mattered--

--you, Mew, and to a much lesser extent Doughnatello my sourdough starter--
Mew

--that's what's irreplaceable. And that all survived just fine.
We're okay, Doreen. We're going to be okay.

I'm choosing to look at it this way: This apartment was a chapter of our lives, and it's done now. So we get to open a new one.
Okay. So tell me this then: What's this new chapter about?

It doesn't work like that. We don't get to just decide.
Hah!
Nah. I'm pretty sure we do.

Come on, let's talk about it! If we're starting a new chapter in our lives, and we can decide what's in it, what do you want it to contain?
Doreen...
What are the three things you can't live without, Nancy Whitehead?

Doughnatello the sourdough starter, you lived a very eventful life before we turned you into delicious bread, and for that we both salute and gobble you.

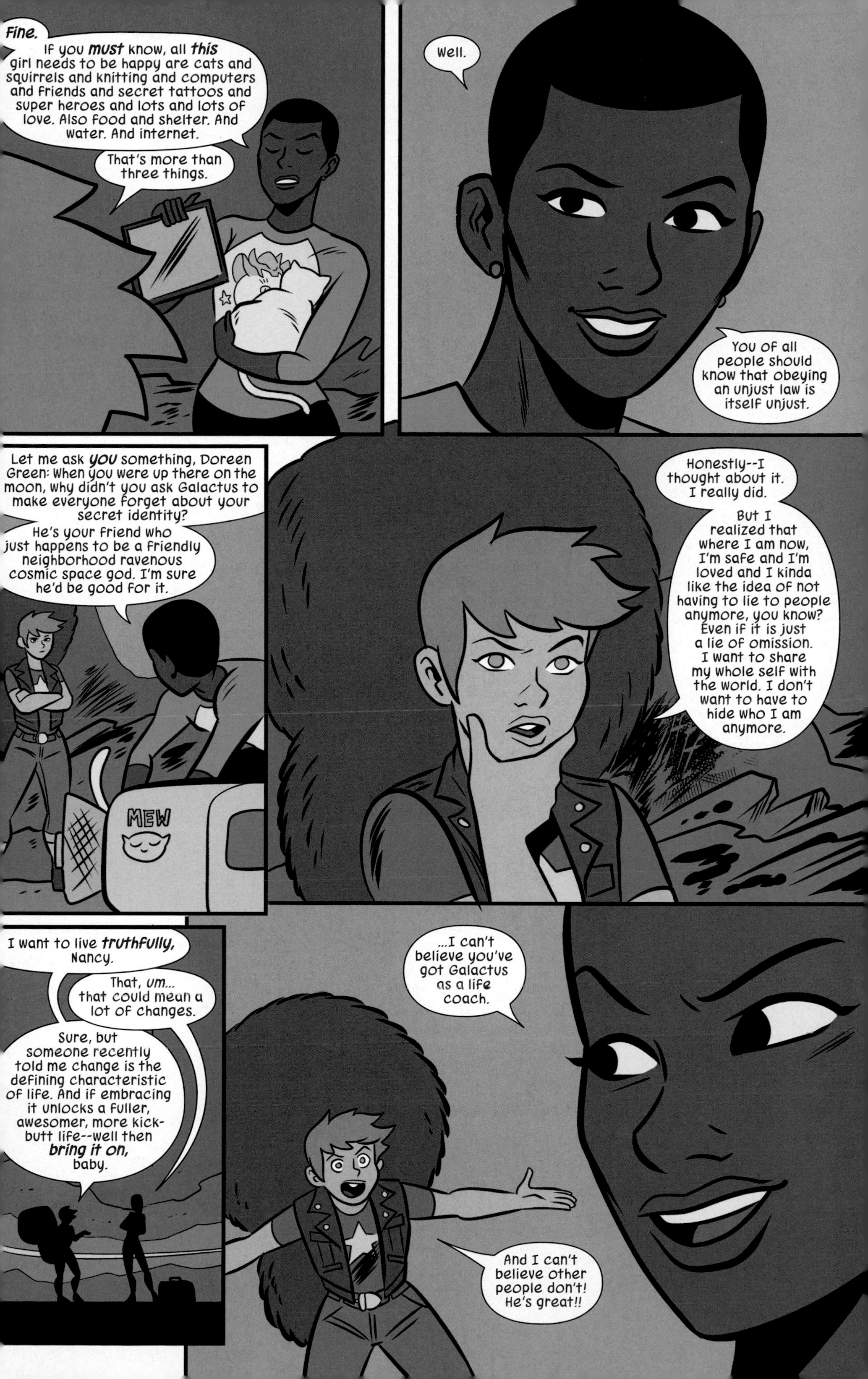
Fine.
If you MUST know, all this girl needs to be happy are cats and squirrels and knitting and computers and friends and secret tattoos and super heroes and lots and lots of love. Also food and shelter. And water. And internet.
That's more than three things.
Well.
You of all people should know that obeying an unjust law is itself unjust.
Let me ask YOU something, Doreen Green: When you were up there on the moon, why didn't you ask Galactus to make everyone forget about your secret identity?
He's your friend who just happens to be a friendly neighborhood ravenous cosmic space god. I'm sure he'd be good for it.
MEW
Honestly--I thought about it. I really did.
But I realized that where I am now, I'm safe and I'm loved and I kinda like the idea of not having to lie to people anymore, you know? Even if it is just a lie of omission. I want to share my whole self with the world. I don't want to have to hide who I am anymore.
I want to live truthfully, Nancy.
That, um... that could mean a lot of changes.
Sure, but someone recently told me change is the defining characteristic of life. And if embracing it unlocks a fuller, awesomer, more kick-butt life--well then bring it on, baby.
...I can't believe you've got Galactus as a life coach.
And I can't believe other people don't! He's great!!

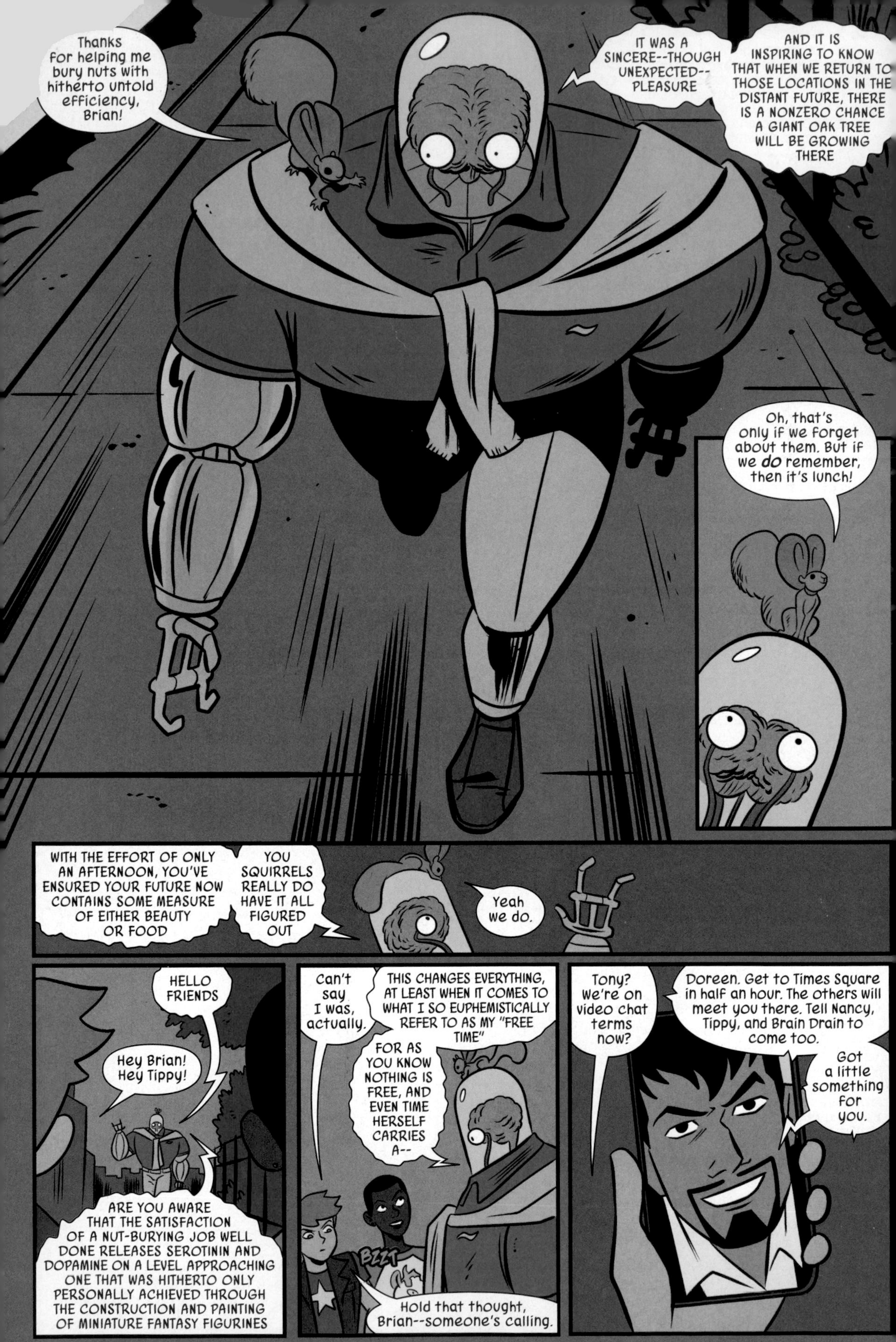

THE PAINTED MINIATURE FANTASY FIGURES CAN THEN BE USED IN TABLETOP GAMING, BUT I ASSURE YOU: THAT ASPECT OF THE HOBBY IS AS OPTIONAL AS IT IS COMPLETELY ENGROSSING AND AMAZING, AND I HAVE NO REGRETS

Wait. How did you know they were all here with me?
Okay *obviously* I've been scraping their location data, but it's for a good cause!
Anthony Edward Stark.
I'll have Jarvis pencil you in for complaints tomorrow at 2. For now, just go to Times Square, all right??
And so...
Okay, this is the time and place, but I don't see Tony anywhe--
BZZZRRRRRT
Wiccan
CLOSING SOON
--and there he is.
Hey, everyone on Earth with a screen. Sorry to interrupt, but paid advertisement here. "I'm Tony Stark, and I approve this message," that whole thing.
By now you've heard about Doreen Green.
I just can't get past how her identity got out. Leaked to cable news? ***Please.*** That's not how you introduce yourself to the world. I mean, I'd do more, but Cap says time travel is wildly unethical, ***"especially*** in my hands." So here's the next best thing:
Historical and CGI deepfaked footage, combined into the best intro video money can buy, set to the official theme tune of my best tailed friend.
Guys, gals, and nonbinary pals...meet Doreen.

DOREEN GREEN, DOREEN GREEN!
GREATEST HERO AND SQUIRREL QUEEN!
SHE'LL CATCH WHO STOLE YOUR PURSE
AND SAVE THE UNIVERSE!
THAT'S WHYYYY
WE ALL LOVE DOREEN GREEN!
IS SHE TOUGH?
LISTEN GOON:
SHE'S HELD MJOLNIR ON THE MOON!
WITH HER FRIENDS BY HER SIDE, EVILDOERS WILL BE DENIED!
AND PLUUSSSSSSS, BRAIN DRAIN IS IN THERE TOO
10: STOP DOING CRIMES 20: GOTO 10
HELLO

SHE KNOWS HOWWWWW TO CODE, AND SHE KNOOOOOWS HOW TO FIGHT
KLIKETY KLAK
AND WHEN DAAAAANGER SHOWS, SHE'LL DEFEND ALL THAT'S RIIIIGHT!
DOREEN GREEN, DOREEN GREEN!
SHE'S THE SQUIRREL GIRL YOU'VE PROBABLY SEEN!

CAN SHE BEAT THANOS DEAD?
SHE'D BEFRIEND HIM INSTEAD!

AND THENNNNNN, HELP HIM WITH ALL HIS ISSUES
THEY'D GO THROUGH SO MUCH TISSUES

BUT THAT'S OUR DOREEN GREEN!
EATS NUTS, KICKS BUTTS
Thank you.
fin.

Doreen Green doesn't just study computer science - she also studies **justice**, thanks to her being born with all the powers of a squirrel **and** all the powers of a girl! With the help of her best friends (human and squirrel), she fights crime and saves Earth on the regular. Her pals call her Doreen - which means you can too! - but if you ever see her in costume, keep her secret identity safe and call her...**The Unbeatable Squirrel Girl!**

Squirrel Girl *in a nutshell*

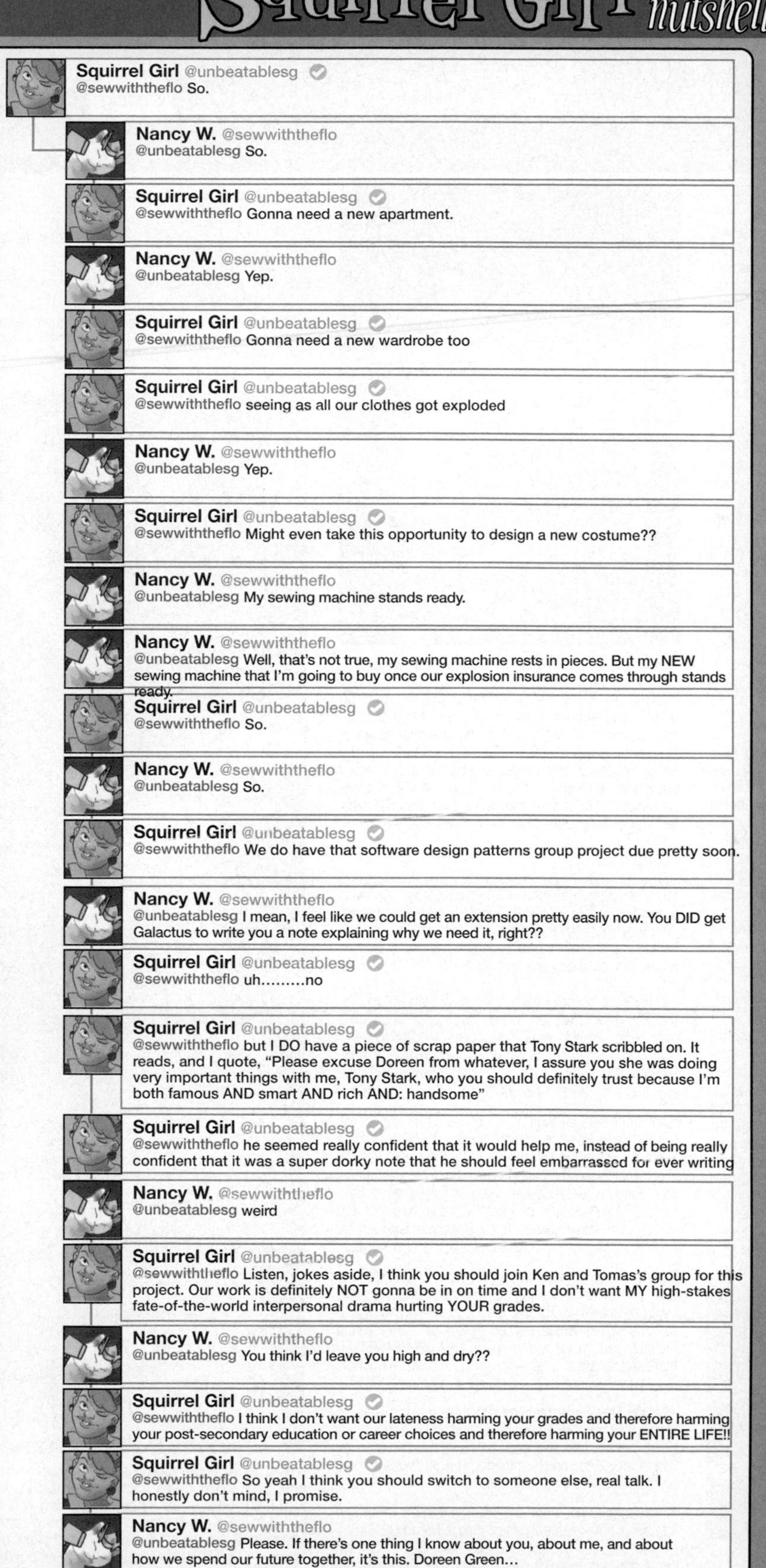

Squirrel Girl @unbeatablesg
@sewwiththeflo So.
Nancy W. @sewwiththeflo
@unbeatablesg So.
Squirrel Girl @unbeatablesg
@sewwiththeflo Gonna need a new apartment.
Nancy W. @sewwiththeflo
@unbeatablesg Yep.
Squirrel Girl @unbeatablesg
@sewwiththeflo Gonna need a new wardrobe too
Squirrel Girl @unbeatablesg
@sewwiththeflo seeing as all our clothes got exploded
Nancy W. @sewwiththeflo
@unbeatablesg Yep.
Squirrel Girl @unbeatablesg
@sewwiththeflo Might even take this opportunity to design a new costume??
Nancy W. @sewwiththeflo
@unbeatablesg My sewing machine stands ready.
Nancy W. @sewwiththeflo
@unbeatablesg Well, that's not true, my sewing machine rests in pieces. But my NEW sewing machine that I'm going to buy once our explosion insurance comes through stands ready.
Squirrel Girl @unbeatablesg
@sewwiththeflo So.
Nancy W. @sewwiththeflo
@unbeatablesg So.
Squirrel Girl @unbeatablesg
@sewwiththeflo We do have that software design patterns group project due pretty soon.
Nancy W. @sewwiththeflo
@unbeatablesg I mean, I feel like we could get an extension pretty easily now. You DID get Galactus to write you a note explaining why we need it, right??
Squirrel Girl @unbeatablesg
@sewwiththeflo uh.........no
Squirrel Girl @unbeatablesg
@sewwiththeflo but I DO have a piece of scrap paper that Tony Stark scribbled on. It reads, and I quote, "Please excuse Doreen from whatever, I assure you she was doing very important things with me, Tony Stark, who you should definitely trust because I'm both famous AND smart AND rich AND: handsome"
Squirrel Girl @unbeatablesg
@sewwiththeflo he seemed really confident that it would help me, instead of being really confident that it was a super dorky note that he should feel embarrassed for ever writing
Nancy W. @sewwiththeflo
@unbeatablesg weird
Squirrel Girl @unbeatablesg
@sewwiththeflo Listen, jokes aside, I think you should join Ken and Tomas's group for this project. Our work is definitely NOT gonna be in on time and I don't want MY high-stakes fate-of-the-world interpersonal drama hurting YOUR grades.
Nancy W. @sewwiththeflo
@unbeatablesg You think I'd leave you high and dry??
Squirrel Girl @unbeatablesg
@sewwiththeflo I think I don't want our lateness harming your grades and therefore harming your post-secondary education or career choices and therefore harming your ENTIRE LIFE!!
Squirrel Girl @unbeatablesg
@sewwiththeflo So yeah I think you should switch to someone else, real talk. I honestly don't mind, I promise.
Nancy W. @sewwiththeflo
@unbeatablesg Please. If there's one thing I know about you, about me, and about how we spend our future together, it's this. Doreen Green...
Nancy W. @sewwiththeflo
@unbeatablesg ...you're not getting rid of me that easily. <3

search!

Letters From Nuts

Derek!

Hi!

I have been reading SQUIRREL GIRL for well over a year now, and when I found out the series was ending I was devastated. I always like to say that I am this world's equivalent of Squirrel Girl minus a few minor details. I am a second-year computer science student (and I love reading the code included in the comic); I too am a girl and have all the powers of a girl; we have a similar haircut; I try to befriend everyone; and I love a good puzzle (that's probably the computer science part coming back into play, but it counts as two different things!). Honestly, the differences aren't too big when you look at all the similarities. I do not have a tail, or the powers of a squirrel for that matter; I don't have a group of super hero friends to go fight crime with, nor do I have a really cool squirrel friend. So sadly I'm not completely Squirrel Girl — yet.

In all seriousness, however, books like SQUIRREL GIRL are insanely important to our world and I am so glad I got to be a part of this audience. To see women like Doreen Green and Nancy Whitehead going out and finding their own way to be themselves and save the world time and time again is so empowering to people everywhere. So thank you all for every ounce of creativity you have poured into this 50-issue run and thank you for telling Doreen's, Nancy's, Monkey Joe's, Tippy Toe's, Brain Drain's, Mew's, Kraven's, Tomas', and Ken's story to all of us these past years.

Kira

RYAN: Kira, with the CS skills and everything else, what does a little (okay, not-so-little) tail and Squirrelese knowledge matter? I say: NOT MUCH. Thank you so much for this, and thank you for being a part of it! That maybe sounds like a line, but it's sincere here: This book wouldn't exist (and wouldn't have continued to exist) without readers like you getting into it, sharing it, and eating nuts and kicking butts. So WELL DONE to Team Doreen, all of us.

DEREK: Kira, this is so great to hear. Thank you so much for reading and being the secret, real-world Doreen Green!

Hi Ryan and Erica,

Our daughter Maya really got into reading SQUIRREL GIRL with us last year, and she helped get her whole pre-K class into it too! Her awesome teacher Ms. Holmes developed a big end-of-year project where the whole class put together a comic book about a blue alien named Cammie. The kids learned from local experts about the steps needed to make a comic book and then they each contributed to the book. Here are some pictures. (Maya is the blond one in red showing off her SQUIRREL GIRL book.) Thanks for inspiring such a cool experience!

Cheers,
Maya and parents Michelle and Evan

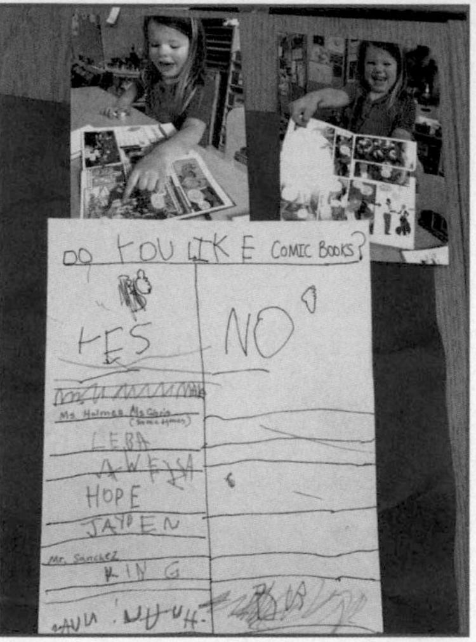

RYAN: Oh my gosh, there is so much to love here. I think I love...EVERYTHING about this? A whole class of pre-kindergarten kids making comics is SO GREAT, and what a legacy to have a small part in. Also: I love that Maya is reading the choose-your-own-path issue of SQUIRREL GIRL (already in the deep, nonlinear end of the sequential arts!), and I completely love that on the "who loves comics" sign-up sheet, there is only one name that was CLEARLY put there by accident and scribbled out. Amazing!

Hi, Squirrel Scouts!

I've been following Doreen and pals' adventures for nearly a year now, and I have to just say that you guys are amazing. Who knew that a single girl (okay, and some squirrels) could beat Doctor Doom? I mostly have been reading in graphic novel form, but then I switched for the War of the Realms.

For my 10th birthday party, I threw a Marvel Gaming-themed party (part of it we just spent squabbling over who would win, Deadpool or Squirrel Girl, until I showed them SQUIRREL GIRL BEATS UP THE MARVEL UNIVERSE) just so I could dress up as the one and only Doreen Green! I've put a picture below.

After all of that, me and a few of the same friends (hi, Rachel, Harry, Harrison, and Ned!) started writing a comic book! It's called We Haven't Decided The Name Yet. It's about four super heroes (Twister, Goldock, Vampirella, and Crysto) who decide they want to have a super hero team but can't decide the name! I'm the illustrator and letterer, and thanks, Derek, Erica, Ryan, and Rico for my inspiration! My style is roughly based on Derek's, so yeah.

Back in January, I went skiing in Japan. For the first time ever, I went down the second-hardest run there was! I was so scared for the big drop. I closed my eyes and thought, "What would Doreen Green do?" She would probably just go for it and shout, "NO REGRETS!!!" So that's exactly what I did. And I made it down the whole run, in a snowstorm, without falling! Yahooo!

After all of this, I was heartbroken to hear that this series is ending this run. I'm sure whoever will take over will be great, but no one will ever be as groundbreaking as Ryan, Derek, Erica, and the others. :(But, on the bright side, we'll always have the memories.

Since I'm originally from England, me and my mum find it hilarious how in America the comic is THE UNBEATABLE SQURL GRL, not THE UNBEATABLE SQUIRREL GIRL!! But since I'm now living in Hong Kong, I've been learning Mandarin. Squirrel Girl is 松鼠女孩, or Sōngshǔ nǚhái. Genuine translation! You just learned Chinese!!

Thank you for an amazing comic!

Nuts,
Abby
Hong Kong

P.S. Chuk chuk ckrrr churrrrr!!

P.P.S. Here are some squirrely photos of me as Squirrel Girl and our comic book!!

P.P.P.S. Could we please, please have more Gwenpool team-ups? I loved it. Also could you do a team-up with Shuri, please?

P.P.P.P.S. Okay, I'll stop with the P.S.es now!

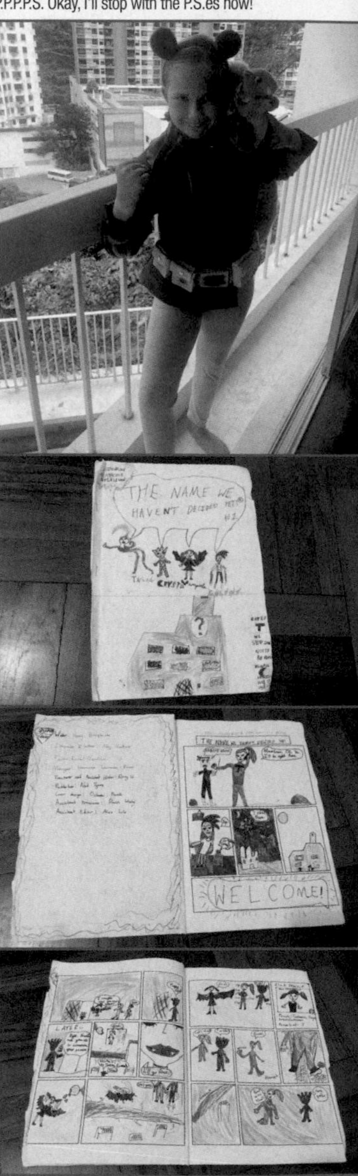

RYAN: Oh my gosh, your skiing story. I have a similar one, from when I was younger and hadn't written SQUIRREL GIRL — or much of anything yet! I was going to do a jump around a blind corner, and this snowboarder had just parked himself right on the ramp — a ridiculously stupid place to sit down! So I couldn't avoid him in time and clipped him with one of my skis, which then disengaged and left me with just one, hurtling toward the ramp. I thought, "I could sit

down and end this," but in the moment part of me thought, "OR, I could do this jump anyway and land it on ONE FOOT and be the most amazing ever and probably it won't hurt too bad if you mess it up!" Anyway I did it, and I landed it, and then I stopped and made the snowboarder toss me my ski. I like to think he was impressed. This has nothing to do with Doreen, but now you all know that I did a cool ski move once!! I love your costume, and I'm envious of your traveling and Mandarin-learning, and my advice is to both continue to make comics but also to hold on to them! I've lost all the early comics I made, and I wish I hadn't.

DEREK: Abby, thanks so much! Glad to know the Mandarin translation for Squirrel Girl! Both your costume and your comic are amazing, and I agree with Ryan: Keep your comics as you make them! That way you can always look back and see how far you've come or get inspired by ideas you'd forgotten about!

Hi, Amazing People Who Make Doreen Green a Reality!

As THE UNBEATABLE SQUIRREL GIRL is nearing its end, I just wanted to thank all of you for this series. It was one of the first comics I read when I was getting into comics in college, and it has been really special to me. I have since finished college with degrees in neuroscience, film, and... COMPUTER SCIENCE, and the motivation to keep at it was thanks in no small part to books like SQUIRREL GIRL, where you showed people who were passionate about CS but also had other interests and passions (namely, fighting crime). I know it sounds kinda hokey, but getting to see Doreen & co. doing that has helped me realize that we CAN balance diverse aspects of our lives, and that being into STEM doesn't mean you can't also like other stuff (for me, it's art and writing). It's also inspiring me to seriously try to make my own comics, so thanks, and I hope all of you keep making awesome, inspiring things for eons to come!!!

Brian T. Sullivan, 24
Ft. Collins, CO

RYAN: Brian, I am so in favor of your degrees! I graduated with a degree in computer science and a minor in film, so all I needed was some neuroscience to pull together the BRIAN ACHIEVEMENT SET. Maybe one day! The reason I did that minor in film was for the same reasons you're probably feeling: I didn't want to do just one thing. I wanted balance, and I wanted to be a guy who liked computers but also liked other things too (or alternatively, a guy who liked stories but also liked computers too). It wasn't easy at times (and it didn't help that I was the only one in the program doing that), which means I'm so glad I could be some inspiration in this, and I can't wait to see what you do next!!

DEREK: Knowing what I now know about what happens when the powers of computer science and comics are combined, I also can't wait to see what you come up with!

Hi Ryan and Derek,

My name is Ava and I am your #1 fan (I'm not kidding!). You two are the greatest (and Erica too — I'm so sad that you left!). Last year on Halloween, I dressed up as Squirrel Girl, and everyone loved it! I wore my costume again today to a comic con, and this little girl came up to me and said, "Mommy, look, it's Squirrel Girl — I want a picture!" I can see why everyone loves her; she is friendly, nutty, and squirrely.

Every month I look forward to getting my subscription copy in the mail; thank you for making Squirrel Girl!

Ava D.
St. Paul, MN

RYAN: Ava! It is always a pleasure to meet a #1 fan (in my head you are all tied for first, this is canon). That costume is amazing and I'm glad that in that moment, when that little girl wanted a photo with Squirrel Girl, you got to feel what it's like to be her. Thank you for reading!!

DEREK: Thanks so much, Ava! Hope you enjoyed this last issue! Your Squirrel Girl costume is amazing, but that giant Tippy is especially amazing!

Dear Nutty Crew,

Yesterday was a very happy day for my two children — 12-year-old daughter Jones and 9-year-old son Dash — because I presented them with the latest Squirrel Girl book, "Call Your Squirrelfriend," purchased from our favorite comic shop, Kings Comics in Sydney.

But it was also a very sad day because I had to inform them that I'd just learned SQUIRREL GIRL was ending with issue #50.

My kids — especially Jones — were upset at the news because they have loved reading your comic from the very beginning. In fact, last year Jones dressed up as her favorite hero for her school's Book Week celebrations (photo attached).

While it's sad to see SQUIRREL GIRL go, Jones and Dash want to thank everyone involved — especially Ryan, Erica, and Derek — for bringing so much reading pleasure and joy to them (oh…and to me too, because people of ALL AGES can love SQUIRREL GIRL).

All the best from Down Under (where we have no squirrels, but some pretty darn feisty possums).

The Lennard clan (Jones, Dash, Dann, and Helen)
Sydney, Australia

RYAN: How is every Squirrel Girl costume so good? It seems impossible, and yet, it's true. Well done, Jones!! A situation like this, in which a whole family can read and enjoy the book, was what we were shooting for when we first pitched this all-ages Squirrel Girl book over five years ago, and it's so great to see that realized. And now, when Jones and Dash get the last book, finish the story, and turn to the last page, they'll get to see their letter here. Hey there, Lennard clan! Thanks for being awesome, and thanks for reading! <3

DEREK: So many great Squirrel Girl costumes in this column! Thanks so much to the whole Lennard clan!

Dear Team Doreen,

This is the best comic ever. I just want to say that right off the bat because it's true. Squirrel Girl was my first Marvel Comic (because there was *Tiny Titans* and *Batman: Li'l Gotham* to prepare me), and it has remained seriously the best, out of THOR (Jane Foster run, obviously), MS. MARVEL, CAPTAIN MARVEL (from "Higher, Further, Faster, More" to "Alien Nation," which are three different series), IRONHEART, SPIDER-GWEN, and THE UNSTOPPABLE WASP...although those are basically all tied for second place, to be fair.

Speaking of the Wasp, why have Nadia and Doreen not teamed up yet? Yeah, Nadia's been busy with A.I.M. and other stuff, but Doreen's been single-handedly saving North America in WOTR!!! They both have the "hang on, why are we even fighting" vibe, and they would be best-friend science ladies having science adventures forever. In fact, why isn't Nadia part of MARVEL RISING?

I love this comic. It has taught me how to count on my fingers in binary (still waiting for someone to ask me about this), how to be empathetic toward super villains, and also why squirrels, koi, and chipmunks are nature's overlooked powerhouses, in the words of Ken. You also taught me about silent/invisible/not actually real EMPs, which miiiiiiight just appear in a really important moment in the book I'm writing. The main character is the same percent geek as me (approximately 1,000,000,000%), which means that I get to make a really obscure USG reference every three seconds!

Let's get real, though: This comic has influenced my perspective of the world, and my life in general, soooo much. I have a friend named Ava (hi, Ava!) who is a Squirrel Scout alongside me, and I'm pretty sure that she is secretly a super hero and is punching criminals as I type this. We bonded over Marvel — specifically, USG! I lend her all my comics, and I want to literally never stop. Just like YOU should never stop printing! I know, I know, issue #49 comes out tomorrow and the series ends at #50, but every other cool lady super hero's comic ended and then rebooted, like, next month, so — fingers crossed! Ryan, you have to keep writing Doreen. I'm serious; you're the only person who ever treats her seriously. Erica and Derek, you're the best artists, and I want to see more of your work in every comic. EVERY comic. This whole team taught me how to draw/write comics/books/really random cartoons.

All right, this letter is getting really long. I hope you read this, even if you run out of space/time and it doesn't get published. Don't forget: Even after this series, don't be afraid to get nuts. In fact, get more nuts than anyone has yet dared to achieve.

Nutty till the end,
Sophia Werthmuller

(P.S. Enclosed is one of my USG sketches. And yes, that IS a "Felicitations to the Sister, I Am Whale" T-shirt. And yes, whoever is in charge of merchandise must print them immediately in compensation to Squirrel Scouts for the end of the comic.)

RYAN: Sophia, thank you! I loved the sketches and all the USG symbols in them. Thank you for all the super-kind words, and I do love how I've gotten lots of messages like this from you and other people that said things like, "Hey, listen, Ryan, if you decided to change your mind and keep doing SQUIRREL GIRL, we wouldn't even be mad. Just in case you were thinking of doing that: It'd be super fine." It's very flattering!! Nadia and Doreen (and Shuri) not teaming up is one of the things I regret I never got around to, though we did discuss it at different times…but this way it's possible for you to say, "Wow, how courteous of the current creative team to leave room for future artists and writers to tell new stories! Their magnanimity is exceeded only by their humble brilliance!!" So let's go with that reading, and I look forward to reading one of your books one day, Sophia!!

DEREK: Thanks, Sophia! I've also learned so many fun facts and skills from this book that I'm just waiting for the opportunity to unleash on people! LOVE the drawing and especially the shirt! Thank you also for the last-minute advice; consider it taken!

Attention, Squirrel Scouts! Thanks for checking out our production blog, **unbeatablesquirrelgirl.tumblr.com**, where we posted behind-the-scenes stuff, along with all sorts of cool things *you* made. And thanks for reading this comic! Y'all are the best! Keep eating nuts and kicking butts!

Farewells From Nuts

This (as you hopefully already know, otherwise sorry for breaking the news to you so abruptly!) is the final issue of our run on SQUIRREL GIRL — which includes 58 issues, two number ones, two number 50s (if you count #42 as the 50th-issue celebration, WHICH I DEFINITELY DO), plus a graphic novel. All told, that's over 1,260 pages of UNBEATABLE SQUIRREL GIRL (or 10011101100 pages if you're counting in binary, WHICH WE DEFINITELY ARE). And for a large percentage of you, that's that same number of pages that you've read, shared, laughed, cried, and pumped your fist in the air and said "YES!" to. (Probably not all at the same time, but…maybe??) It turns out *War and Peace* is a mere 1,225 pages, so we're weighing in at 1.03 Tolstoys here. What I'm saying is: *We did good.* We're the longest-running current book in the Marvel Universe. Books don't reach #50 nowadays. *This wasn't supposed to happen.*

I have a lot of complicated feelings about leaving the book. You probably do too! Some of you were reading all sorts of comics for decades before picking up this series, while others have literally *learned* how to read on this here funny book! It's hard to say goodbye, especially to a comic like this, something that changed my life and let me work with so many amazing people, like Erica and Derek and Rico and Travis and Wil and Sarah. And I don't know precisely what happens next. None of us do, really!

But I do know a few things. I know I'll write more comics in the future — and if you ever see a book out there with "RYAN NORTH" (and/or any of our names!) on the cover, maybe give it a look! We'll be there waiting for you.

I also know that there will come a time, maybe soon, when there'll be another comic with Squirrel Girl in it. She won't be quite the same, of course. But then again, like Galactus says, neither will we. And maybe one fine day — if we haven't already — you and I will meet each other at a convention or a talk or just on the street, and that shared history — of comics, of this book, of Doreen and Nancy and Tippy and Mew and Kraven and Brain Drain and Galactus and the rest — it'll tie us together. It already has.

I'm going to miss this, I'm going to miss us, and I can't wait to see what happens next.

To Wil, who told me way back when that you "always saw Doreen as someone who helped people." Squirrel Girl is who she is because of who you are.

To Sarah, who gave great suggestions, made great catches, and who highlighted puns I put in the script and simply commented "Ryan." It's how I knew I was doing a good job, and you can't spell "Ryan North" without "Ryan no."

To Erica and Derek and Rico and Travis: We started out as people assigned to work together by a multinational corporation and became actual for-real good pals, and I'm so happy that aside from everything else, one of the lasting legacies of this book is the friendship we share. You couldn't ask for a better ending than that.

And finally, to the hundreds of thousands of you who have bought Doreen's comics or taken them out from the library or passed around a beat-up issue in the schoolyard between classes: thank you. We just make the comics. You're the ones who make everything else possible.

-Ryan

-Erica

Goodbye for now, everyone! Thanks so much for reading, drawing fan art, making costumes, writing in, and caring so much about this series. This book was special, and the people involved put so much into every page — it was really an amazing thing to be a part of for these past 18 issues. I already miss it but am proud of this big complete chunk of comics that we can now revisit, and I'm looking forward to seeing these characters pop up elsewhere in the Marvel Universe and beyond! <3

-Derek

UNBEATABLE SQUIRREL GIRL has been a blast to color. I'll miss both the team of wonderful characters in the books and the team I made them with. Every USG fan I've met at a library, comic shop, or comic convention has been wonderful. Thanks so much for coming along on Doreen and her friends' adventures, and thanks to all the new friends I made along the way. Too cheesy?

-Rico

I can't wait until my daughter can start reading SQUIRREL GIRL. Inside the pages of these comics, she will read about a strong super-powered hero whose strength isn't really her muscles or powers at all — it's her caring, friendship, and intelligence that most often save the day. Doreen Green and her pals have a view of the world that sees opportunity for change and growth in those whom others may condemn as only a "villain." Anti-cynical, brave, funny, smart, and tough when necessary…that's the hero I was happy to put word balloons and sound effects next to for these past years. And I'm really looking forward to sharing those adventures with my daughter as she learns to read and learns to be unbeatable. Thanks a bunch to Ryan, Erica, Derek, Rico, Sarah, and Wil! Now on to the next adventure!

-Travis

ISSUE #50 VARIANT COVER BY **RAHZZAH**

Each month, Marvel publishes a catalog announcing its upcoming releases. **Ryan North** wrote the catalog copy for all 58 issues of ***THE UNBEATABLE SQUIRREL GIRL*** (plus the graphic novel!), and since they're as charming and funny as everything else Ryan writes, we thought we'd include all of them here — along with Erica Henderson's wonderful covers — as a special bonus!

THE UNBEATABLE SQUIRREL GIRL #1

RYAN NORTH (W)
ERICA HENDERSON (A/C)

• Wolverine, Deadpool, Doctor Doom, Thanos: There's one hero who's beaten them all — and now she's got her own ongoing series! (Not that she's bragging.)

• That's right, you asked for it, you got it, it's SQUIRREL GIRL! (She's also starting college this semester.)

• It's the start of a brand-new series of adventures starring the nuttiest and most upbeat super hero in the world!

THE UNBEATABLE SQUIRREL GIRL #2

RYAN NORTH (W)
ERICA HENDERSON (A/C)

• Starting college is hard enough, but now Squirrel Girl has to deal with Galactus too?

• The fate of the entire planet hangs in the balance, and only Squirrel Girl can save it!

• Also, her squirrel friend Tippy-Toe. She can help too.

• Iron Man might show up too! Kinda, at least!

THE UNBEATABLE SQUIRREL GIRL #3

RYAN NORTH (W)
ERICA HENDERSON (A/C)

• Time is running out, and the only way for Squirrel Girl to stop Galactus is to get to the moon...you know, somehow??

• See the unveiling of Squirrel Girl's new Flying Squirrel Suit...that she maaaaybe borrowed from Iron Man.

• Also, the final face-off with Galactus! ON THE MOON.

THE UNBEATABLE SQUIRREL GIRL #4

RYAN NORTH (W)
ERICA HENDERSON (A/C)

• The final showdown between Galactus and Squirrel Girl is here!

• It's the Power Cosmic versus the Power Chestnut: WHO WILL WIN?

• Also, Squirrel Girl is late for class. So there're TWO disasters coming!!

THE UNBEATABLE SQUIRREL GIRL #5

RYAN NORTH (W)
ERICA HENDERSON (A/C)

• The breakout character of 2015 continues her one-woman crusade against injustice and jerks in this stand-alone issue, a perfect jumping-on point for new readers!

• These TAILS of the Squirrel Girl will show you the Marvel Universe's most powerful super hero from a bunch of brand-new perspectives, several of them QUITE ASTONISHING.

• This comic is actually a bunch of mini comics in one, giving it definitely the #1 most-comics-per-actual-physical-comic value in stores today!!

THE UNBEATABLE SQUIRREL GIRL #6

RYAN NORTH (W)
ERICA HENDERSON (A/C)

• The start of a new arc! Squirrel Girl meets some potential new allies, including... GIRL SQUIRREL??

• I don't know why we put question marks there; it's actually what happens!

• Also a hippo named "Hippo" is in this issue! This character already existed and we absolutely did NOT make him up at the last minute!

• ALSO THERE'RE FIGHTS!! AND EVEN SOME FEELINGS!

THE UNBEATABLE SQUIRREL GIRL #7

RYAN NORTH (W)
ERICA HENDERSON (A/C)

• Our friend Squirrel Girl doesn't like our new friend Girl Squirrel! In this issue we'll discover if this dislike is...POTENTIALLY JUSTIFIED??

• Also: If you don't care whether or not these two people like each other, perhaps me telling you that THE WORLD HAS GONE MAD AND SQUIRREL GIRL HAS TO FIGHT THE AVENGERS IN THIS ISSUE will attract your attention?

• It did? Well guess what: She also fights Ratatoskr, the Norse God of Squirrels!

• Also, Old Guy Thor is in this issue! As is New Lady Thor! We don't have Frog Thor, though.

• That seems like an oversight, actually??

THE UNBEATABLE SQUIRREL GIRL #8

RYAN NORTH (W)
ERICA HENDERSON (A/C)

• It's the classic tale of good (squirrel) versus evil (squirrel) as SQUIRREL GIRL fights RATATOSKR, the Norse Squirrel God! The fate of the world hangs in the balance!

• And yes, "Norse Squirrel God" means that Thor shows up to help! AND Loki!

• Loki's a huge character! He's been in THREE different movies so far. Three!

• He's only in our comic for a couple of pages though.

• Oh! This book also features FRIENDSHIP and SASS and PUNCHES!!

THE UNBEATABLE SQUIRREL GIRL #1

RYAN NORTH (W)
ERICA HENDERSON (A/C)

NEW SERIES. NEW AVENGER(!). STILL EATS NUTS AND KICKS BUTTS!

Galactus. Thanos. M.O.D.O.K. With her unique combination of wit, empathy and totally kick-butt squirrel powers, Doreen Green — A.K.A. the Unbeatable Squirrel Girl — has taken ALL these chumps down! Alongside her friends Tippy-Toe (a squirrel) and Nancy (a regular human with no powers whatsoever — they checked), Squirrel Girl is all that stands between Earth and total destruction! Sometimes. Other times there're no threats and she's just a regular computer science student. That's an adventure too though!

THE UNBEATABLE SQUIRREL GIRL #2

RYAN NORTH (W)
ERICA HENDERSON (A/C)

• Remember last month when we said #1 was a great jumping-on point for new readers? Well, guess what? Issue #2 is too! Start of a new story, baby!

• (It's ALSO a great "continuing-on" point for existing readers.)

• In this issue, Squirrel Girl gets sent BACK IN TIME and also ERASED FROM HISTORY. Only her friend Nancy even remembers she existed!

• So Nancy turns to the only hero she can contact (on social media) for help in rescuing her: IRON MAN.

• Also a surprise villain shows up from the past! It could be LITERALLY ANY BAD GUY, but it's a good one, I PROMISE.

• P.S.: It is not Galactus; we already did him.

THE UNBEATABLE SQUIRREL GIRL #3

RYAN NORTH (W)
ERICA HENDERSON (A/C)

• Squirrel Girl has woken up only to find she's been hurled back in time to the 1960s! Mondays, am I right?

• And if that wasn't trouble enough, her friend Nancy is coming face-to-face with the villainous [CENSORED]!

• Yes, I've noticed that when I type [CENSORED]'s name it shows up as [CENSORED]; no, I don't know how to fix that.

• This book features the following: Squirrel Girl, time travel, [CENSORED] and emotions! It promises to satisfy fans of each of those things, even if they don't like the other things!

• Which is great because emotions are just THE WORST.

THE UNBEATABLE SQUIRREL GIRL #4

RYAN NORTH (W)
ERICA HENDERSON (A/C)

PREVIOUSLY ON "THE UNBEATABLE SQUIRREL GIRL":

• Squirrel Girl is trapped in the past, and friend Nancy has gone back to rescue her!

• But Nancy didn't have a time machine, so she hitched a ride with DOCTOR DOOM!!

• So now it's Squirrel Girl versus Doctor Doom in the 1960s, fighting for the fate of the very planet!! What could possibly go wrong, right??

• Well anyway, in this issue EVERYTHING GOES WRONG FOREVER.

THE UNBEATABLE SQUIRREL GIRL #5

RYAN NORTH (W)
ERICA HENDERSON (A/C)

• Squirrel Girl has been sent back in time to the '60s, which would be fine I guess, except now the future is ruled by Doctor Doom!

• Anyway, that's not her fault, but she's still fixing it because she's just THAT GOOD.

• The final battle between Doctor Doom, Squirrel Girl and...an old-lady version of Squirrel Girl from the future?? Yes! Meet the sensational character find of 2016: AN OLD LADY!

• Fun fact: Besides adults literally fighting each other, this issue also features SEVERAL jokes!

• Don't miss the hit comic featured on *Entertainment Weekly*'s Must List (which was several months ago for everyone reading this, but it was just yesterday when this text was being written and we're all still very excited about it!)!

THE UNBEATABLE SQUIRREL GIRL #6

RYAN NORTH &
CHIP ZDARSKY (W)
ERICA HENDERSON &
JOE QUINONES (A/C)

PART ONE OF "ANIMAL HOUSE," A CROSSOVER WITH HOWARD THE DUCK!

• Squirrel Girl and Howard will team up against an enemy that neither Squirrel Girl (who has defeated Galactus) nor Howard the Duck (who has defeated...uh...well, listen, I'm sure he's got other qualities) could take down on their own!

• Will they fight over a trivial misunderstanding? Will they band together against a common enemy? Will Squirrel Girl say, "Duck!" to mean "lower your head" but Howard will misinterpret it as a call for his attention, leading him to get hit on the head by something?

• At least ONE of those three questions will be answered with a "yes" in this issue!

• CONCLUDED NEXT MONTH IN HOWARD THE DUCK #6!

HOWARD THE DUCK #6

CHIP ZDARSKY &
RYAN NORTH (W)
JOE QUINONES &
ERICA HENDERSON (A/C)

THE CONCLUSION OF "ANIMAL HOUSE," A CROSSOVER WITH THE UNBEATABLE SQUIRREL GIRL!

• WATCH! Howard show Squirrel Girl how to be a REAL hero for a change, for which she is eternally grateful!

• LEARN! what happened in last month's UNBEATABLE SQUIRREL GIRL #6 from the recap page!

• LISTEN! to a nice audio file of nature sounds made by Chip and Ryan while you read this VERY good story!

• LOVE! all the guest stars! Like one of the blue guys from X-MEN! And a pretty cool van!

THE UNBEATABLE SQUIRREL GIRL #7

RYAN NORTH (W)
ERICA HENDERSON (A/C)

a) This special issue, called "BE THE UNBEATABLE SQUIRREL GIRL," puts YOU in control of THE MOST POWERFUL CHARACTER IN THE MARVEL UNIVERSE. Will you fight crime and save the day? Or will you be a complete jerk and use her powers to tell everyone off?

b) I'm serious: These are actual choices, and you have to make them RIGHT NOW! To be Squirrel Girl and fight crime, turn to c). To be Squirrel Girl and be a jerk instead, turn to e).

c) Well, you're in luck vis-à-vis crimefighting, because Squirrel Girl is going to be facing off against SWARM, a bad guy made out of bees! And that's not all. To learn more about the other bad guys she can face, turn to d)! But if INSTEAD you'd like to stop reading this and get excited about this book and maybe order it, please: feel free!

d) Nice try, but we've got to keep SOME surprises for the book! You decide to definitely buy this comic and see who they are. THE END.

e) What? No, why would you even want to be a jerk? Geez, man, maybe this ISN'T the comic for you. Turn to b) and answer better this time!

THE UNBEATABLE SQUIRREL GIRL #8

RYAN NORTH (W)
ERICA HENDERSON (A/C)

NEW STORY STARTS NOW!

• In this story, Squirrel Girl faces off against a giant monster AND a gross old man AND goes on some dates!

• So that's three challenges right there

• Whether you're a fan of seeing a squirrel lady punch someone OR a fan of seeing a squirrel lady struggle to make an online dating profile that isn't weird and embarrassing, this is an excellent comic for you to purchase!

• EVERYONE IS ONE OF THOSE TWO TYPES OF PEOPLE — search your heart and you will find it is true.

• Oh P.S., the story is called "I KISSED A SQUIRREL AND I LIKED IT" — how amazing is that?

• Answer: very.

THE UNBEATABLE SQUIRREL GIRL #9

RYAN NORTH (W)
ERICA HENDERSON (A/C)

• The comic that got TWO #1s in its first year now reaches a new milestone: its very first #9!

• In Part 2 of "I Kissed a Squirrel and I Liked It," Squirrel Girl's date with a chump gets interrupted by MOLE MAN, who is a man who lives underground and can't see that well! Hence the name!!

• Squirrel Girl is really good at empathizing with bad guys and talking them down, but what happens when she's TOO good at that?

• Buy this comic to find out, because we show exactly that taking place! Spoiler alert: There're punches AND jokes.

• Not a dream! Not an imaginary story! ONE of the following three things WILL ACTUALLY OCCUR in this issue! 1) A pleasant visit to a coffee shop with friends; 2) A man with fishy powers suggests using fish to solve a problem, big surprise; 3) SQUIRREL GIRL USES HER TAIL TO KNOCK THE SMIRK RIGHT OFF A DUDE'S FACE!!

• Haha, whoa, I hope it's the third one.

THE UNBEATABLE SQUIRREL GIRL #10

RYAN NORTH (W)
ERICA HENDERSON (A/C)

• Mole Man has fallen in love with Squirrel Girl, and he's holding the world hostage until she goes on a date with him!

• MOLE MEN, am I right??

• Watch as Squirrel Girl gains the help of an unlikely ally! Thrill as two people kiss! BUT WHICH TWO??

• You'll have to buy the issue to find out, so all I'll say right now is this:

• IN THIS ISSUE THERE IS A NON-ZERO CHANCE FOR EVERY MARVEL SHIP TO BECOME CANON!!

• "Ship" is short for "relationship," in case you thought I was talking about, like, Galactus' "Star Sphere" or Mr. Fantastic's "Fantasticship" or whatever.

• Anyway, enjoy!!

THE UNBEATABLE SQUIRREL GIRL #11

RYAN NORTH (W)
ERICA HENDERSON (A/C)

• This special one-off issue promises two amazing things: SUPER HEROICS and COMPUTER SCIENCE.

• Yes! By the end of this issue, you will know both how Squirrel Girl can take down COUNT NEFARIA and also a few really fundamental concepts in computer science!

• Have we found a way to express CS concepts through the medium of super hero fights? YOU'LL HAVE TO ORDER THE ISSUE TO FIND OUT!

• But yeah, we totally did.

• Featuring all the greatest Squirrel Girl tropes you love! Including fights, jokes and COLD, HARD LOGIC.

THE UNBEATABLE SQUIRREL GIRL #12

RYAN NORTH (W)
ERICA HENDERSON (A/C)

• Everyone gets a weeklong break from class, and Squirrel Girl is taking Nancy to visit her parents up in Canada! WHAT COULD POSSIBLY GO WRONG, RIGHT?

• Turns out, nothing! It's a great trip and nothing of note happens and our comic is actually EXTREMELY DULL. Sorry, everyone.

• No, just kidding! Our comic is actually SUPER AWESOME and things get real crazy real quick once a certain super-powered villain nobody has heard of for over a decade reappears!

• That's right! This comic features mysteries AND Canadians AND camping, not to mention our ALREADY super-enticing focus on squirrel powers!

• Let's see Howard the Duck promise you THAT.

THE UNBEATABLE SQUIRREL GIRL BEATS UP THE MARVEL UNIVERSE OGN-HC

RYAN NORTH (W)
ERICA HENDERSON (A/C)

Proof that we're living in the best of all possible worlds: Marvel is publishing a Squirrel Girl graphic novel! It's a stand-alone adventure that's great for both old fans and new readers! It's a story so huge it demanded an original graphic novel! It's a story so nuts it incorporates both senses of that word (insanity and squirrel food)! And it's the best! Squirrel Girl kicks butts, eats nuts, talks to squirrels and also punches really well. She has defeated Thanos, Galactus and Doctor Doom (twice!). But now she'll encounter her most dangerous, most powerful, most unbeatable enemy yet: herself! Specifically, an evil duplicate made possible through mad science (both computer and regular) as well as some bad decisions. In other words, Squirrel Girl beats up the Marvel Universe! YES!

THE UNBEATABLE SQUIRREL GIRL #13

RYAN NORTH (W)
ERICA HENDERSON (A/C)

• SOMEONE is taking over the continental United States, but Squirrel Girl is stuck in boring ol' Canada! UH-OH.

• Canada's not actually that boring, though: Did you know we have the world's longest covered bridge, in Hartland, New Brunswick? It's true! I've seen it!

• It's pretty long, I GUESS.

• Anyway, enough about Canada, we're here to find out why you should buy this comic! REASONS INCLUDE: fights, teamwork, continental USA domination and a special guest star who you'll find a TINY bit familiar? Everyone is at least a LITTLE bit into this guy and I CAN'T imagine you not being excited to

discover who it is!
• Anyway, yeah, it's Ant-Man.

THE UNBEATABLE SQUIRREL GIRL #14

RYAN NORTH (W)
ERICA HENDERSON (A/C)

• Squirrel Girl and Ant-Man! It's the team-up you probably NEVER thought you'd see!

• Although, if you thought about it for a bit, you probably WOULD expect to see it at some point, since they both hang out with tiny animals and are both super heroes.

• Honestly, I'm a little surprised it hasn't happened sooner.

• Anyway, besides squirrels (adorable) and ants (so tiny, so bitey), this issue also includes wrestling AND philosophy. YES. Finally, am I right??

• I am prepared to say this is the #1 BEST COMIC you can buy that features squirrels, ants, wrestling and philosophy!!

• I am also prepared to say that this is the ONLY comic you can buy that features these four things, but heck, we all have to be the change we want to see in the world, right?

THE UNBEATABLE SQUIRREL GIRL #15

RYAN NORTH (W)
ERICA HENDERSON (A/C)

• When the TASKMASTER comes to town — and brings with him his ability to DUPLICATE ANYONE'S SWEET MOVES — who stands between him and total domination?

• See, I can tell you're glancing at the title of this comic and whispering "Well, it's PROBABLY Squirrel Girl," but guess what? This time it's actually Nancy's cat, Mew, who has NO POWERS WHATSOEVER!

• THRILL as Mew loafs around the house! GASP as Mew chases a mouse and then has a nap! BOGGLE as you wonder how we possibly managed to pitch "an issue entirely from the cat's point of view" to Marvel, a multinational corporation with a LOT invested in our comic continuing to star a squirrel and/or girl!

• They knew the risks when they let Hawkeye have that Pizza Dog issue though, so this was clearly inevitable.

• MEW ISSUE, BRING YOUR TISSUES!

THE UNBEATABLE SQUIRREL GIRL #16

RYAN NORTH &
WILL MURRAY (W)
ERICA HENDERSON (A/C)

• It's the 25th anniversary of Squirrel Girl! Twenty-five years ago THIS MONTH, she made her first appearance in MARVEL SUPER-HEROES vol. 2 #8, way back in January 1992!

• Then nothing really happened with her for like a decade, until 2005, when she appeared in — wait, what am I, Wikipedia? Wikipedia has all this stuff, and people don't read comic solicits for a HISTORY LESSON: They read them for some SWEET SPOILERS on what will be in their comics several months from now! So let's spoil some comics, huh??

• SPOILERS BEGIN. In celebration of 25 years of Squirrel Girl (SEVERAL of which actually featured the publication of comics starring her), we've brought back Squirrel Girl's co-creator, Will Murray, to write only his SECOND Squirrel Girl story ever!

• It's Squirrel Girl's 15th birthday, and she's gotten the greatest present of all: a run-in with THE INCREDIBLE HULK??

• Also, your regular Squirrel Girl team is here to also tell a story, so that's cool too (Erica's drawing both)!

• Two stories, two writers, one artist and one quarter of a century with a character! It's a special one-shot you won't want to miss!!

• SPOILERS OVER. Now try to act surprised when you read it, okay??

THE UNBEATABLE SQUIRREL GIRL #17

RYAN NORTH (W)
ERICA HENDERSON (A/C)

• It's a normal quiet day at Empire State University, filled with lots of lectures and higher education, and OH BOY, I can already hear y'all buckling up for a jam-packed thrill ride of students learning quietly!!

• Well, BAD NEWS on that front, friends: Once all that quiet learning is out of the way, there's gonna be a FISTFIGHT!

• Plus, besides the cool fistfight, Doreen ALSO gets a new FLYING SQUIRREL suit, making her easily 2150% more unbeatable!

• With a new more powerful Squirrel Girl and a rad new suit, I'm certain crime is over forever. There's definitely not a new super villain in town conspiring to mold Squirrel Girl into the perfect minion...

• ...OR IS THERE? Who can say? Heck, I guess the only way to know for sure is to buy the comic and find out, right?

THE UNBEATABLE SQUIRREL GIRL #18

RYAN NORTH (W)
ERICA HENDERSON (A/C)

• Squirrel Girl has met a mysterious benefactor who has given her a flying squirrel suit that's definitely reliable and trustworthy! All is fine in the world, yes?

• You may be saying, "Yes, of course, and it certainly sounds like this is going to be a refreshingly calm and event-free issue of my favorite talking squirrel comic," but if you'll recall what the last few pages of our previous issue dramatically revealed, you'll remember that, no, we're actually all in a lot of trouble!

• Squirrel Girl is being manipulated by someone whose motivations nobody knows; Nancy is struggling with a challenging programming problem off-panel (which is why you didn't see it in the last issue, but don't worry, she'll figure it out); AND a chicken named Alfredo is in a high-stakes battle for his very life!

• Gasp at a secret invasion of character motivations! Thrill at a chaos war of emotions! Boggle as monsters truly get unleashed and Doreen's fate hangs in the balance!

• Squirrels and girls and punching, oh my!

THE UNBEATABLE SQUIRREL GIRL #19

RYAN NORTH (W)
ERICA HENDERSON (A/C)

• Worst mentor ever Melissa Morbeck has trapped Squirrel Girl in her house, surrounded by zoo animals under her control, and laid out her demands: She wants to have...A CHAT.

• Does that not sound exciting enough? What if we were to tell you that this chat ALSO involves punching, shocking revelations, a little bit of cool computer stuff and MACHINE-GUN-WIELDING BEARS, who are as extremely cute as they are extremely deadly??

• Squirrels AND machine-gun bears, all in the same comic?! That's right. Only SQUIRREL GIRL gives you what you want, assuming you have those two very particular interests!!

• Hopefully you do; we've got a lot riding on this.

THE UNBEATABLE SQUIRREL GIRL #20

RYAN NORTH (W)
ERICA HENDERSON (A/C)

• This is it! The epic showdown between Melissa and Squirrel Girl as the fate of New York City — and everyone in it — hangs in the balance!

• Will Melissa's secret intentions be uncovered? Will Doreen and her friends be able to stop her? Can squirrels TRULY hope to match an army made up of EVERY OTHER ANIMAL EVER?

• Great news: We have studied each of these questions extremely carefully, and we are pleased to reveal our answers in this upcoming issue of THE UNBEATABLE SQUIRREL GIRL!

THE UNBEATABLE SQUIRREL GIRL #21

RYAN NORTH (W)
ERICA HENDERSON (A/C)

• Squirrel Girl, Nancy and Mary go to the Negative Zone for the weekend! So Koi Boi, Chipmunk Hunk and Brain Drain PROMISE to fight any crimes that pop up so that the city will be just as Squirrel Girl left it when she returns! This would be a very short and uneventful issue, except for these facts:

• A crime wave begins the second Squirrel Girl leaves.

• Koi Boi and Chipmunk Hunk are powerless to stop it, so things get real bad real quick.

• And Brain Drain is a nihilist brain in a jar on a robot body, which means he's KINDA a pain to be around sometimes?

• This special stand-alone issue features friendship, fights and friendship fights! PLUS other things too, but you'll have to buy the issue to find out, because this is just the solicit text and we don't want to spoil everything. Honestly, you probably shouldn't even be reading these solicits unless you own a comic book store because they are chock-FULL of spoilers!!

THE UNBEATABLE SQUIRREL GIRL #22

RYAN NORTH (W)
ERICA HENDERSON (A/C)

• When Doreen Green and Nancy Whitehead enter a mysterious programming competition, they don't suspect that the prize for winners will be...an all-expenses-paid trip to the SAVAGE LAND!

• Yes: THE SAVAGE LAND! Also known as "a mysterious tropical region of Antarctica that we discovered is actually populated by DINOSAURS"!

• In the Marvel Universe, I mean.

• In OUR universe, the only thing ever discovered in that region was a note from Robert Scott's doomed expedition to the South Pole (he arrived there weeks after his competition, Roald Amundsen, got there first), which read in part, "This is an awful place and terrible enough for us to have labored to it without the reward of priority"!

• The story of those Antarctic expeditions is fascinating, but OURS IS PRETTY FASCINATING TOO, plus it has Squirrel Girl AND dinosaurs in it!!

• So maybe read up on the other ones but definitely check out our comic right away.

THE UNBEATABLE SQUIRREL GIRL #23

RYAN NORTH (W)
ERICA HENDERSON (A/C)

• Remember last issue, when we went to the SAVAGE LAND, the nature preserve full of dinosaurs?

• Guess what? We're still in the amazing SAVAGE LAND, and there're even MORE dinosaurs!

• Will Squirrel Girl FIGHT a dinosaur? Will Squirrel Girl fight TWO dinosaurs? Will we come up with really excellent reasons why these fights would take place, reasons that both justify the fights while also telling the story of what led to this dinosaur-punching smash-up: a story which, even though it stars dinosaurs and Squirrel Girls, contains within it the chance for us to recognize, perhaps for the first time, our most personal and secret selves??

• Of course we will; that's literally our job.

• This issue also features jokes and a super villain who's causing major problems, so it's the complete package, really.

THE UNBEATABLE SQUIRREL GIRL #24

RYAN NORTH (W)
ERICA HENDERSON (A/C)

• Squirrel Girl, Nancy and Tippy are trapped in the Savage Land! Good thing there're only regular dinosaurs there and not, for example, a giant metal killer-dinosaur version of Ultron instead!!

• Sorry, I'm just getting word that there is, in fact, a giant metal killer-dinosaur version of Ultron here, and Squirrel Girl needs to stop him before he takes over the world — a task that has regularly bested many other super heroes, including the Avengers themselves!

• But don't worry, because SQUIRREL GIRL IS NOT ALONE: She's got Nancy (a regular human with no powers) and Tippy (a regular squirrel with no powers) on her side to help her out against the rage of Ultron!

• And it's not just any Ultron but a new and improved Ultron with an extremely dangerous (and, we must admit, extremely awesome) Tyrannosaurus rex bod!

• Oh, also Kraven the Hunter is in this issue too, so if you love dinosaurs, robots AND men in lion vests, boy howdy, have we got a comic book for you!

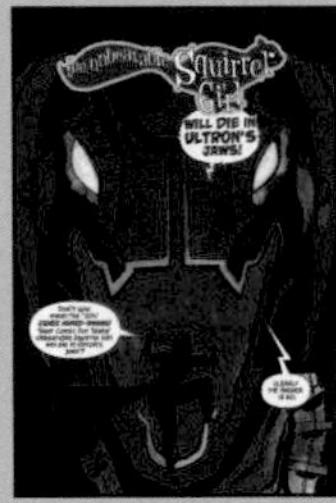

THE UNBEATABLE SQUIRREL GIRL #25

RYAN NORTH (W)
ERICA HENDERSON (A/C)

• This is it! The climactic showdown between SQUIRREL GIRL, a woman who can talk to squirrels, and ULTRON HIMSELF, a killer robot who has ruthlessly defeated the Avengers on multiple occasions!

• And you may be thinking, "Holy crap, I'M SOLD," but let me tell you more: This entire battle takes place in the Savage Land, an area FILLED with dinosaurs!

• And NOW you may be thinking, "I'm so sold, good grief, just let me read this comic already," but hold on some more, because there's one more thing we need to tell you: ULTRON IS A TYRANNOSAURUS REX NOW.

• It's Doreen Green versus DINOSAUR ROBOT ULTRON, and Kraven the Hunter is there too!

• Kraven is not a dinosaur, though.

• Man, we really should've made Kraven a dinosaur too!

• Lesson learned for next time, I guess!

THE UNBEATABLE SQUIRREL GIRL #26

RYAN NORTH with
ERICA HENDERSON (W)
CARLA SPEED McNEIL,
CHIP ZDARSKY,
MICHAEL CHO, RAHZZAH,
RICO RENZI & MORE (A)
ERICA HENDERSON (C)

• In this special stand-alone issue, Squirrel Girl has convinced, cajoled and otherwise induced her friends in the Marvel Universe to make comics of their own! For the very first time, find out what kind of comics your favorite Marvel characters would REALLY make!

• Will Tony Stark write author-insert coffee-shop alternate-reality comics where everyone talks up how great he is? It seems likely, and yet, he has given us something EVEN CRAZIER to publish!

• Featuring TONS of special guest artists, including a legendary comic strip artist making his Marvel debut!

• This unique view of both Squirrel Girl and the Marvel Universe is sure to make readers laugh, turn the page, read a bit, see a new joke and then laugh again! It may also make readers say, "Oh my gosh, you've gotta read this comic; I'm so glad I purchased it at my local comic book store and will definitely patronize them again in the near future!!"

• NO OTHER COMIC is making this explicit promise this month, so in our opinion you should definitely order our talking squirrel comic book.

THE UNBEATABLE SQUIRREL GIRL #27

RYAN NORTH (W)
ERICA HENDERSON (A/C)

THE FORBIDDEN PLA-NUT Part 1

What happens when we take Squirrel Girl back to her roots? Well, we shoot her into space, OBVIOUSLY. Nancy and Tippy find themselves on an alien world where all is not what it seems. Squirrel Girl needs to find a way to get to the other side of the universe to save 'em, STAT. Intergalactic transport through the cosmic realm? This sounds like a job for the Sorcerer Supreme! I'm sure Doctor Strange will be happy to he— I'm sorry, what's that? Doctor Strange is gone and now LOKI is Earth's Sorcerer Supreme? Oh. Well, I'm sure he'll do his best. After all, what could possibly go wrong? Guess what, in this issue, everything possible goes wrong! PLUS: Includes three bonus MARVEL PRIMER PAGES!

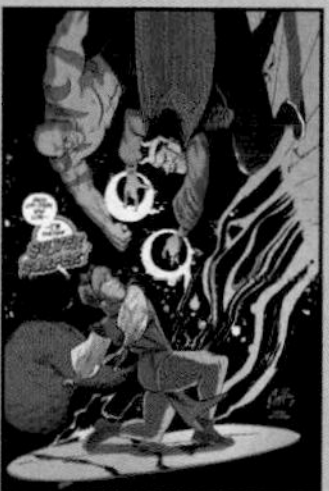

THE UNBEATABLE SQUIRREL GIRL #28

RYAN NORTH (W)
ERICA HENDERSON (A/C)

THE FORBIDDEN PLA-NUT PART 2

• Nancy (human, no powers) and Tippy-Toe (squirrel, no powers) have been kidnapped! Trapped on an alien world filled with alien squirrels, they have only a short amount of time to figure out something — ANYTHING — before EVERYBODY DIES.

• But that's okay, because Squirrel Girl will rescue them, right? I'd love to say, "Yes, absolutely," but instead I am forced to say, "No way, she's trapped on Earth, she barely knows where they are and she has to defeat THE DREAD DORMAMMU before she can go anywhere!"

• And with LOKI standing in as Sorcerer Supreme, it's not like this battle is going to be A) easy or B) at all winnable.

• That's right: Loki's back, baby! Can CAT THOR be far behind?

THE UNBEATABLE SQUIRREL GIRL #29

RYAN NORTH (W)
ERICA HENDERSON (A/C)

THE FORBIDDEN PLA-NUT PART 3

• For the first time in the HISTORY of comics, we present the color-coded fight we've all been waiting for: GREEN (Doreen) ON SILVER (Surfer)!

• And if fighting the Herald of Galactus — a man who literally has the Power Cosmic at his disposal — isn't enough, Doreen's got other problems to deal with, including intergalactic scam artists, Drax the Destroyer and LOKI LAUFEYSON.

• FEEL the thrill of the fight! SEE it happen via artisanally selected images and words juxtaposed in deliberate sequence! HEAR the words in your head via your inner voice as you read them, which when you think about it is kind of weird! All we have to do is write down words on a piece of paper, and suddenly they're re-created in your mind exactly as we intended. Minds are crazy, and language is EVEN CRAZIER.

•Anyway, please enjoy this comic about a girl and her talking squirrel in space.

THE UNBEATABLE SQUIRREL GIRL #30

RYAN NORTH (W)
ERICA HENDERSON (A/C)

• It's the climax (IN SPACE!) of our story as Squirrel Girl (IN SPACE!) faces off against an alien armada (IN SPACE; YES, THIS IS ALSO IN SPACE, THE WHOLE STORY IS IN SPACE!).

• Not just her life hangs in the balance, but also the lives of Tippy, Nancy, Loki, Drax, the Silver Surfer AND an entire planet full of squirrels, so if you believe that stakes can be raised simply by adding more characters into the mix, GOOD NEWS: YOU ARE IN LUCK!

• Will Squirrel Girl survive? Will the alien grifters be brought to justice? Will we see more of Horse Thor, the Thor Who Is Actually a Horse and Who May Have Been Invented Solely for This Solicit Text but Maybe Not?

• Only time, and this comic in particular, will tell!

THE UNBEATABLE SQUIRREL GIRL #31

RYAN NORTH (W)
ERICA HENDERSON (A/C)

• Have you been doodling "I wish they'd do an issue where Squirrel Girl got a new super-power and Nancy Whitehead ALSO got a super-power" in your diary? WE HAVE SOME GOOD, INCREDIBLY SPECIFIC-TO-YOU NEWS: That is happening!

• In this special stand-alone issue, when Doreen and Nancy are blasted into hypertime, they're moving so fast as to be invisible to everyone. So of course they decide to fight crime at super-speed!

• But are there downsides to moving really fast? (Yes, there are.)

• Can anyone in regular time get them back? (Nope.)

• Will they be trapped there...FOREVER??

• We're not answering that last question because you'll have to buy the issue to find out!

THE UNBEATABLE SQUIRREL GIRL #32

RYAN NORTH (W)
DEREK CHARM (A)
ERICA HENDERSON (C)

• Doreen Green (A.K.A. the super hero Squirrel Girl) and her friend Nancy Whitehead (an unrelated civilian) have had a great idea: Let's get some friends together and play an escape room! Escape rooms are those real-life games where you get locked in a room and have an hour to escape before you die!

• In the game, I mean. It's not like if you die in the game you die in real life! Hah hah.

• They gather KOI BOI, CHIPMUNK HUNK, BRAIN DRAIN and, as a special guest...their good friend KRAVEN THE HUNTER.

• BUT WHEN THEY ENTER THE ROOM IT TURNS OUT THAT IF YOU DIE IN THE GAME YOU DIE IN REAL LIFE!! TWIST!!

• It's everything you crave: friendship, adventure and a room full of death traps that you can only find in SQUIRREL GIRL!

THE UNBEATABLE SQUIRREL GIRL #33

RYAN NORTH (W)
DEREK CHARM (A)
ERICA HENDERSON (C)

• Trapped in a deadly room from which the only escape is DEATH, Squirrel Girl and Kraven must try to figure out a way to survive!

• But who is pulling the strings? WHY does someone want them dead? And even if they CAN escape, what guarantee do they have that their troubles aren't just beginning?

• NONE! They have NO guarantees, which is too bad for them but great for YOU, the reader! And it's especially great for you, the reader who is presumably interested in stories of SUPER HERO CONFLICT and SUPER-POWERED FIGHTS!!!

• All that PLUS Brain Drain, Koi Boi, Chipmunk Hunk AND MORE await you in an issue so astounding, so filled with adventure, that we could ONLY call it "The Unbeatable Squirrel Girl Issue 33"!

THE UNBEATABLE SQUIRREL GIRL #34

RYAN NORTH (W)
DEREK CHARM (A)
ERICA HENDERSON (C)

• Squirrel Girl and Kraven have had a nice day out as civilians, instead of their usual costumed identities! It was really straightforward and uneventful...

• ...is what we'd be saying if this was a way more boring comic, WHICH IT ISN'T! Instead we can say that Squirrel Girl and Kraven battled Mojo's evil clone and saved the city from his deadly machinations. Then they all got arrested!

• When Doreen Green and Sergei Kravinoff end up BEHIND BARS, can they be saved? Will they even make it to trial? And who will be their lawyer?

• We can answer that last one: It's obviously going to be none other than JENNIFER WALTERS, the incredible SHE-HULK!

• Doreen behind bars! Kraven on the stand! And a conclusion to the trial that nobody will see coming! It's all this and more in this particular Marvel comic!

THE UNBEATABLE SQUIRREL GIRL #35

RYAN NORTH (W)
DEREK CHARM (A)
ERICA HENDERSON (C)

• Squirrel Girl may have avoided going to jail, but now Kraven's a fugitive on the run! It's been a difficult day!

• Can Squirrel Girl stop Kraven and Spider-Man from fighting before it's too late?

• Can a squirrel named Haskell be a major part of a super hero epic?

• Can Brain Drain use some well-applied existentialist philosophy to save the day?

• The answer to all these questions is, "I dunno, MAYBE?" And you'll have to read the comic to find out anything more specific!

• UNBEATABLE SQUIRREL GIRL #35 is your one-stop shop for a) friendship, b) punching and c) SPIDER-MAN, HE'S BEEN IN LOTS OF MOVIES, EVERYONE LOVES HIM.

THE UNBEATABLE SQUIRREL GIRL #36

RYAN NORTH (W)
DEREK CHARM (A)
ERICA HENDERSON (C)

• Comics have been famously described as "pictorial and other images in deliberate sequence," but do you need words too? Perhaps so, but also...PERHAPS NOT??

• In this special, stand-alone, ALL-SILENT ISSUE of the UNBEATABLE SQUIRREL GIRL, she and Iron Man face off against a villain neither has seen before — who will render them quite literally speechless!

• It's an action-packed adventure that anyone can read, filled with surprises, excitement, action and — for once — NO WORDS!

• This is what Ryan gets for jamming so many words into previous issues.

THE UNBEATABLE SQUIRREL GIRL #37

RYAN NORTH (W)
DEREK CHARM (A)
ERICA HENDERSON (C)

• It's the latest issue of the all-ages smash hit THE UNBEATABLE SQUIRREL GIRL! She's defeated Galactus! She's defeated Doctor Doom! Who KNOWS what fun adventures she'll get up to THIS month!

• Well, we do. And you may want to brace yourselves for this, because this issue begins an all-new story arc called..."THE DEATH OF SQUIRREL GIRL"!

• Has the Unbeatable Squirrel Girl been BEATEN? Is this TRULY the end of Doreen Green? We haven't canceled the comic so it doesn't seem likely, but can you REALLY be sure? What if this issue installment actually IS the one Squirrel Girl dies in and you miss out because you didn't buy it?

• So I guess what we're saying here is everyone should definitely buy this comic.

• PLUS: This issue also has Wolverine in it for LITERALLY several pages!

THE UNBEATABLE SQUIRREL GIRL #38

RYAN NORTH (W)
DEREK CHARM (A)
ERICA HENDERSON (C)

SQUIRREL GIRL IS DEAD!

• ...is what you'd be saying if you only read the cover of our last issue and NOT the contents, in which we revealed a shocking twist: Squirrel Girl...IS ALIVE?

• Yes! The good news is everyone's favorite squirrel-themed super hero is alive and well! But the bad news is: Whoever replaced her...was a shape-shifting alien SKRULL, and now Team Doreen doesn't know who to trust!

• Mysteries deepen and allegiances are tested in this issue as...a shocking Skrull is revealed!

• It's not Nancy, though.

• Nancy's great.

THE UNBEATABLE SQUIRREL GIRL #39

RYAN NORTH (W)
DEREK CHARM (A)
ERICA HENDERSON (C)

• Last issue ended with Squirrel Girl and someone CLAIMING to be Iron Man getting into a fight! Will this issue show you how that fight goes and who wins and why? THE ANSWER: yes!

• But with an Iron Man imposter on the scene, that means the real Tony Stark is missing! It's up to Squirrel Girl and her friends to find Tony before it's too late: for him AND the world.

• Unfortunately for Squirrel Girl — as this comic is within the super hero genre of sequential art, one that relies on high-stakes narrative storytelling filled with twists and turns that result in the world never being the same — what she finds is not what she expects, and the world will never be the same!

• All this plus: Let's say underwater adventure too awaits you in this issue of UNBEATABLE SQUIRREL GIRL!

THE UNBEATABLE SQUIRREL GIRL #40

RYAN NORTH (W)
DEREK CHARM (A)
ERICA HENDERSON (C)

• In the past few issues, Squirrel Girl has "died"! She's fought "Iron Man"! And her world has been invaded by a non-zero number of SKRULLS!

• It's been a crazy ride, but gosh, it sure would be nice to know WHY this is happening, WHO is behind it and WHAT machinations — sinister OR otherwise — that they've been working toward!

• Good news: This issue reveals all! Mysteries are laid bare! Secret origins are revealed! And your friend and mine Squirrel Girl is FINALLY brought back from the dead!

• If, like me, your tastes in serialized literature run toward words and pictures in deliberate sequence, then I'm proud to recommend to you THE UNBEATABLE SQUIRREL GIRL #40!

THE UNBEATABLE SQUIRREL GIRL #41

RYAN NORTH (W)
NAOMI FRANQUIZ (A)
ERICA HENDERSON (C)

• In the past months, Squirrel Girl has battled Kraven, rescued NYC from supernatural silence, kinda maybe died and also fought Skrulls! So now it's time for a nice break…which is why in THIS issue, Squirrel Girl does nothing but watch public domain movies on television!

• That's right! She just sits there! You can kinda see the TV screen over her shoulder in a couple of panels, but that's it! It's really quiet and relaxing and nothing much happens.

• …

• …THAT IS, UNTIL NANCY WHITEHEAD AND ANOTHER E.S.U. STUDENT BY THE NAME OF PETER PARKER ARE TAKEN HOSTAGE BY A SUPER VILLAIN INTENT ON PROVING THAT SHE'S THE SMARTEST PERSON ON THE PLANET!

• Then it's super hero battles featuring THOR and SHE-HULK on a DATE! SQUIRREL GIRL matching wits against MS. QUIZZLER! And MORE!

• Artist Naomi Franquiz makes her MARVEL DEBUT in a stand-alone adventure you won't want to miss!

THE UNBEATABLE SQUIRREL GIRL #42

RYAN NORTH (W)
ERICA HENDERSON, DEREK CHARM,
NAOMI FRANQUIZ (A)
ERICA HENDERSON (C)

CELEBRATING 50 ISSUES OF SQUIRREL GIRL!

• It's the 50TH ISSUE of THE UNBEATABLE SQUIRREL GIRL! That's right: this issue — #42 — is our 50th!

• It says #42 on the cover, but that's only because we had eight issues and then a second #1 in our first year, although this of course doesn't count the OGN (SQUIRREL GIRL BEATS UP THE MARVEL UNIVERSE), which is another five issues of story, which would put us at…issue #55? This is getting complicated. Anyway!

• By a certain way of counting, it's our 50TH ISSUE of THE UNBEATABLE SQUIRREL GIRL!

• And to celebrate, we're doing a stand-alone story in which she takes on none other than…KANG THE CONQUEROR. It's a battle across space AND time as Kang attacks three distinct eras of Doreen!

• And it's not just Kang who is joining us for this celebration! Original UNBEATABLE artist Erica Henderson is joining series regular Derek Charm, along with Naomi Franquiz!

• THIS IS A REALLY GOOD ISSUE AND WE'RE SUPER BIASED BUT WE THINK YOU SHOULD ORDER IT, THANKS.

THE UNBEATABLE SQUIRREL GIRL #43

RYAN NORTH (W)
DEREK CHARM (A)
ERICA HENDERSON (C)

WAR OF THE REALMS TIE-IN!

• You know how Squirrel Girl has stayed out of most Marvel events? Turns out, that was only because THOSE events didn't involve her good pal LOKI LAUFEYSON!

• When Earth is attacked as part of the WAR OF THE REALMS, Squirrel Girl is called back from her Negative Zone vacation, and Loki recruits her as part of a secret mission!

• Is Loki running a scheme? Probably. Is he playing a trick? Almost certainly. But he NEVER lies about the safety of his good friend (and Cat Thor creator) Nancy Whitehead, and that puts him and Doreen on the same side.

• It's Squirrel Girl's first BIG EVENT CROSSOVER…but it's still the start of a stand-alone epic that you can still enjoy even if you only read SQUIRREL GIRL!

• Also if you're reading this because you're thinking, "Hmm, I'm big into WAR OF THE REALMS but do I really need to see what happens in SQUIRREL GIRL?" then let me say WOW, DO YOU EVER, THERE'S A REVEAL ON THIS LAST PAGE THAT'S BEEN IN THE WORKS FOR YEARS!

THE UNBEATABLE SQUIRREL GIRL #44

RYAN NORTH (W)
DEREK CHARM (A)
ERICA HENDERSON (C)

WAR OF THE REALMS TIE-IN!

• The other nine realms have fallen, Earth is under attack and the only one who can save us is DOREEN GREEN, A.K.A. THE UNBEATABLE SQUIRREL GIRL.

• So that's terrific. We're in great hands and don't need to worry at all! Phew.

• Or at least we would be, if it weren't for the complicating factor of an ancient Asgardian squirrel chaos god who's decided she wants to be…FRIENDS??

• In this issue, Squirrel Girl and Ratatoskr fight Frost Giants…and their unspoken assumptions about each other!

• This arc is a "WAR OF THE REALMS" TIE-IN, but it's also an awesome stand-alone story that you don't need to be reading all the other comics to get!

• Don't tell Marvel.

THE UNBEATABLE SQUIRREL GIRL #45

RYAN NORTH (W)
DEREK CHARM (A)
ERICA HENDERSON (C)

WAR OF THE REALMS TIE-IN!

• The historic team-up of Ratatoskr — Asgardian chaos squirrel god — and Squirrel Girl — Midgardian squirrel, uh, girl — has not gone well!

• Well, that's not technically true: it's gone well for Ratatoskr, who now has a human identity to play with…but this team-up hasn't technically saved anyone yet.

• And now it probably never will! Squirrel Girl realizes that Ratatoskr isn't playing by the rules, and they split up!

• But can one girl save all of North America? And does one Asgardian chaos squirrel god have machinations going on beneath the surface?

• Answers to these questions, plus fights, plus friendship, plus Frost Giants, PLUS some public domain poetry all await you! THERE IS NO MORE ALLURING A SENTENCE THAN THE ONE WE JUST TYPED. WE CHECKED, THIS IS IT!

THE UNBEATABLE SQUIRREL GIRL #46

RYAN NORTH (W)
DEREK CHARM (A)
ERICA HENDERSON (C)

A WAR OF THE REALMS TIE-IN!

The MOST squirrel-centric WAR OF THE REALMS tie-in reaches its conclusion! Only one woman stands between the invading army of the Frost Giants and utter disaster on Earth, and that woman is SQUIRREL GI— hold on... hold on, sorry. I'm getting word that not one but TWO women actually stand between the Giants and utter disaster on Earth, and one of them is...RATATOSKR?? It seems unlikely that the Norse god of gossip would be on Team Doreen, let alone a valuable member of it — but hey, stranger things have happened, right?

I can't think of any off the top of my head, but they've probably happened. Can SQUIRREL GIRL team up with her SMACK-TALKING ENEMY? Can two people who couldn't be more different find a common ground in time to save everyone? And will BRAIN DRAIN make it back from the Negative Zone?? You may THINK you know the answers to these questions, but only by purchasing and then reading this illustrated picto-narrative will your suspicions be confirmed or denied!

THE UNBEATABLE SQUIRREL GIRL #47

RYAN NORTH (W)
DEREK CHARM (A)
ERICA HENDERSON (C)

BRAIN DRAIN IS MISSING!

• Do you want the good news or the bad news first?

• Let's do the good news: It's the start of a new Squirrel Girl arc! BRAIN DRAIN is missing! A sinister face from the past returns! And the hitherto UNBEATABLE Squirrel Girl will have to face CERTAIN DEFEAT to save him!

• Now the bad news: While this is the start of a new Squirrel Girl arc, it's the start of our LAST Squirrel Girl arc! We're going out on a high note. You have been amazing, and making this book has been amazing, but sadly in four months, THE UNBEATABLE SQUIRREL GIRL will end with issue #50. I KNOW.

• Now the good news again: Because it's our last story ever we're making it COMPLETELY HUGE AND AMAZING, and it is going to BLOW YOUR MIND!

• It's the start of the most nuts Squirrel Girl story ever as lives hang in the balance, narrative threads are resolved, and shocking reveals are made!

• <3

THE UNBEATABLE SQUIRREL GIRL #48

RYAN NORTH (W)
DEREK CHARM (A)
ERICA HENDERSON (C)

• Things go from bad to worse as Brain Drain is still missing and the greatest villains in Marvel history team up to take out the one thing that's stood in their way: our hero, Doreen Green!

• With Melissa doing everything she can to destroy Squirrel Girl, is there anything Doreen can do to survive??

• Gosh, I sure hope so because it'd be nice if we actually make it to #50 BUT TECHNICALLY YOU NEVER KNOW!!

• Especially when Squirrel Girl's first villain, DOCTOR DOOM, is involved...

• I don't want to say more because SPOILERS, but trust us when we say this is a bonkers issue in which bonkers things happen, and you should definitely order it right now!!

THE UNBEATABLE SQUIRREL GIRL #49

RYAN NORTH (W)
DEREK CHARM (A)
ERICA HENDERSON (C)

IT'S THE PENULTIMATE ISSUE OF SQUIRREL GIRL!

• It's also the ULTIMATE issue of Squirrel Girl, at least until the next and last one comes out.

• Wait, I'm getting word that's what "penultimate" means — okay, never mind.

• In this issue: Squirrel Girl faces off against her archnemesis with just some friends and a dressed-only-in-his-underwear Tony Stark at her side. Can she win??

• See, normally you'd say, "Yes, of course she can, it's right there in the title," but this is our second-last issue! ANYTHING CAN HAPPEN!

• INCLUDING SHOCKING TWISTS!!

• Please enjoy the several (SEVERAL) shocking twists in this issue, including the (already established as shocking) return of a beloved character!

THE UNBEATABLE SQUIRREL GIRL #50

RYAN NORTH (W)
DEREK CHARM (A)
ERICA HENDERSON (C)

• This is it! After 58 issues (comics numbering is, dare we say: nuts) an OGN and a whole bunch of both eating nuts AND kicking butts, THE UNBEATABLE SQUIRREL GIRL reaches its 50th and final issue!

• When we say "THE UNBEATABLE SQUIRREL GIRL's final issue" though, we mean the *comic book*, not the character. Doreen Green will be fine! She's fine!

• ...OR IS SHE? Because in our previous issue it really seemed like things WEREN'T fine and since it's our last issue maybe we're feeling that since anything COULD happen then anything SHOULD happen!!

• There's only one way to find out, and you're looking at a solicit text for it!

• Friendship, explosions and friendships forged during explosions: It all comes down to this!!

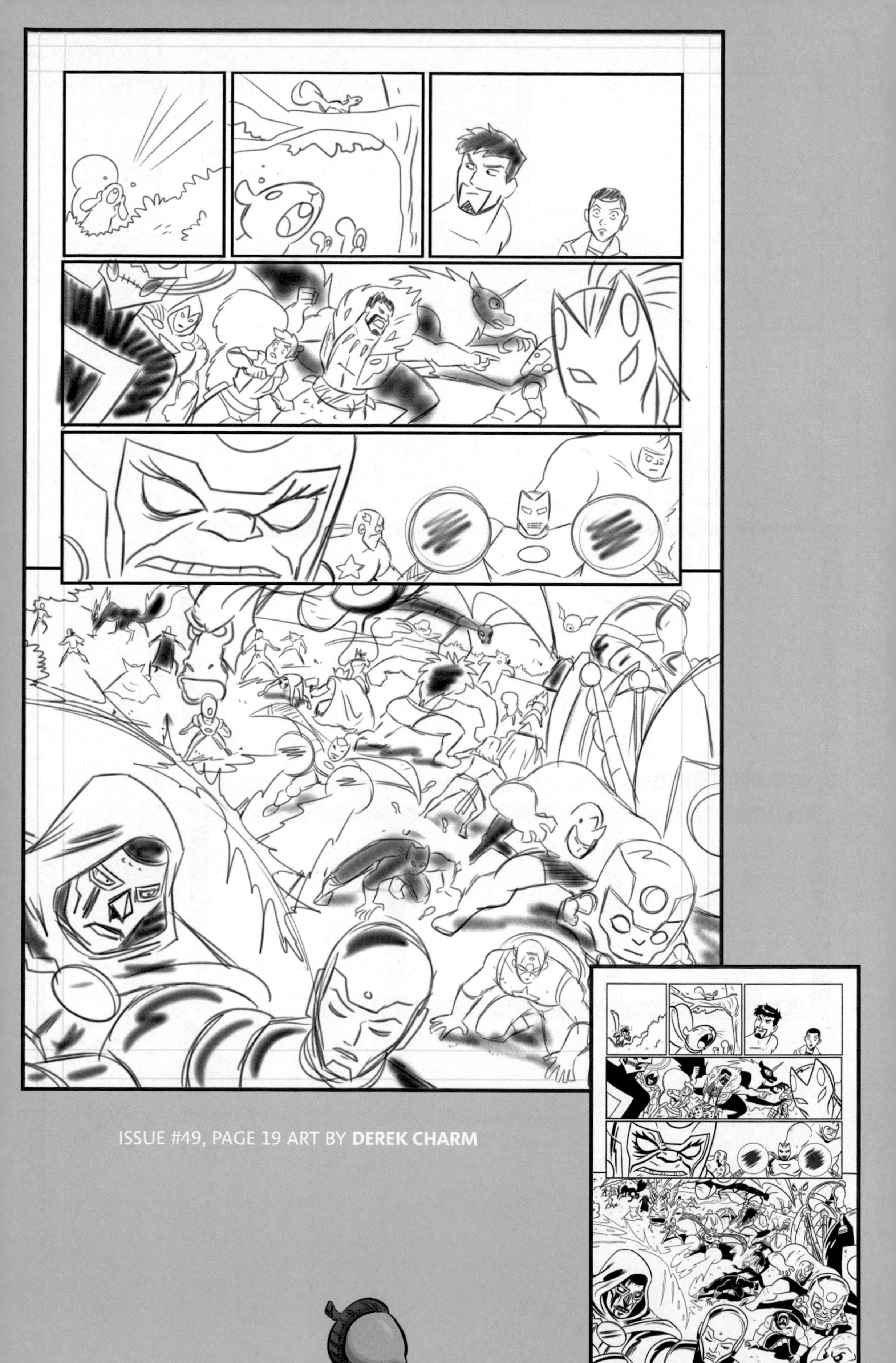

ISSUE #49, PAGE 19 ART BY **DEREK CHARM**

ISSUE #49, PAGE 20 ART BY **DEREK CHARM**